WordPress Web Hosting

How To Use CPanel
and
Your Hosting Control Center

By

Matthew Pitt &
Kent Mauresmo

http://BestWebHostingInc.com

Copyright

Distributed & Published by
Read2Learn.net

Legal Terms

Disclaimer & Terms Of Use

Contents

INTRODUCTION 1

CHAPTER 1. 3

WHAT IS CPANEL? 3

TYPES OF WORDPRESS HOSTING 4

SEARCHING FOR WORDPRESS WEB HOSTING 6

MY TOP 3 RECOMMENDED WORDPRESS HOSTS 7

DO YOUR OWN RESEARCH 11

WHAT TYPE OF CUSTOMER SUPPORT IS AVAILABLE? 11

HOSTING POLICIES AND GUARANTEES 12

SPECIAL OFFERS 13

CHAPTER 2 15

WELCOME TO CPANEL 15

GO DADDY USERS 21

CHAPTER 3 24

CPANEL PARTNERS & PREFERENCES 24

PARTNERS 24

PREFERENCES 25

GO DADDY 28

CHAPTER 4 30

EMAIL 30

GO DADDY MAIL (HOSTING CONTROL CENTER) 35

CHAPTER 5 43

FILE MANAGEMENT AND FTP ACCOUNTS 43

GO DADDY USERS 54

CHAPTER 6 57

STATISTICS 57

CHECK YOUR STATISTICS WITH GO DADDY 65

CHAPTER 7 71

Security 71

Security Features for Go Daddy Users 75

CHAPTER 8 78

Domain Management 78

Go Daddy Domain Management 85

CHAPTER 9 92

Database Tools 92

Go Daddy Database Tools 97

CHAPTER 10 100

Software/Services 100

Advanced 102

Go Daddy Advanced Features 105

CHAPTER 11 106

Website Builders 106

Go Daddy Website Builders 108

CHAPTER 12 109

Upgrades, Professional Services, and Promotional Extras 109

Professional Services 111

Promotional 113

Go Daddy Upgrades, Professional Services, and Other Tools 114

More Tools and Promotions for Go Daddy 115

CHAPTER 13 119

Brief Summary and Conclusion 119

GLOSSARY 121

ACKNOWLEDGMENTS 124

MORE BOOKS FROM THE AUTHORS 125

LINK TO PDF BOOK 126

"Download The PDF Book"

At the end of this book, you'll find a link to download the full color **PDF** copy for free.

Introduction

My name is Matthew Pitt and I run the website www.BestWebHostingInc.com. This book is targeted towards business owners that need help choosing a WordPress hosting provider and using cPanel.

There are hundreds of WordPress hosting providers, and the process of choosing the best web host is very confusing. The goal of this book is to **help you** choose the best WordPress host for your business. After you choose a hosting provider, we'll give you a quick overview showing you how to use important web hosting features to improve your website.

Many popular web hosts use software called **cPanel**. cPanel looks intimidating at first glance, but it's actually very easy to use. We'll help you get familiar with cPanel along with the most important features that you'll use the most.

Some web hosts don't offer cPanel for shared hosting. For example, Go Daddy offers a "**Hosting Control Center**" which is similar to cPanel. We'll show you how to use your "Hosting Control Center" too if you're a Go Daddy user.

The main reason we're writing this book is to help you avoid the same mistakes that we've made. WordPress is so easy to use that most people rarely log into their hosting account. Most WordPress settings can be handled directly through your WordPress dashboard; but your hosting provider has important features that can dramatically improve your website.

If you're new to WordPress hosting, then you'll find this book extremely useful. Since this book is targeted specifically towards WordPress users, we'll focus mainly on the web hosting features relevant to WordPress.

This easy to read book is a **beginner's guide**. If you've been using WordPress and cPanel for several years, then you probably won't learn anything new from this book. If you've recently purchased Kent Mauresmo's book "*How to Build a Website with WordPress...Fast!*" then you'll find this book very useful.

Here are a few things you'll learn from this book:

- What's Cpanel
- How to find Cpanel WordPress hosting
- Types of hosting
- Important features: Disk Space, Bandwidth, MySQL Databases

- Web hosting support
- How to get free domain names
- Referral programs
- Reseller Accounts
- Policies (money back guarantees, shared hosting polices, adult websites, etc.)
- How to create professional email accounts
- How to use sub-domains
- How to use FTP clients
- How to check activity on your websites and error logs
- How to back up your website manually
- SSL certificates
- How to create and use parked domains and a lot more…

This short book is fast paced and very easy to read. We've also included a lot of images in this book to help you learn the material faster. If you're having a problem seeing the images clearly, then jump to the end of this book and **download the PDF** book instead.

If you need additional help after reading this book, please feel free to contact myself or Kent Mauresmo. If you're ready to discover how to easily use your WordPress hosting account and cPanel, let's get started!

Chapter 1

What is cPanel?

cPanel stands for "control panel." cPanel is a software that helps you easily manage your WordPress website and hosting account. You can use cPanel to:

- Managing website files
- Setting up email accounts & auto responders
- Create Sub Domains
- Create Parked Domains
- Create Add-on Domains
- Check Web Stats, and a lot more

cPanel software is one of the most popular web hosting control panels. cPanel offers a user friendly point-and-click interface that'll help you customize your WordPress website and create professional email accounts.

Go Daddy offers similar a software for shared hosting called **HCC** (hosting control center.) Both software's offer similar features, but the layout is different. I'll discuss the setting for both **cPanel** and **Go Daddy's Hosting Control Center** because a lot of people use Go Daddy as well.

The most useful feature that cPanel and HCC offer is the "One-Click Applications" feature. The "One-Click Applications" feature will allow you to easily install WordPress on your web hosting account. All you have to do is answer a few questions and click the "install" button.

You should now have a basic idea of what cPanel is. The next step is to find a web host that offers cPanel and also specializes in WordPress web hosting. In the next section, I'll help you put together a list of web hosts that specialize in WordPress hosting.

It's very important to choose the best WordPress hosting provider based on your needs. If you choose the wrong host, you'll end up wasting a lot of time and money. In the next section we'll discuss:

- Types of hosting
- Important features

- Technical support
- Special features
- Policies

Types of WordPress Hosting

If you don't have a WordPress hosting provider yet, then I'll give you a few tips to help you choose the right host. Before you choose a web host, you need to understand the differences between the 3 basic types of web hosting:

- Shared Hosting
- VPS Hosting
- Dedicated Hosting

Shared Hosting

The most popular type of web hosting is "Shared Hosting." Shared hosting means that there are many websites hosted on a single server. Shared hosting is the cheapest type of web hosting because multiple website owners are sharing the cost of the server.

If you plan on starting a small to medium sized website, then shared hosting will be the best option for you. If you're also starting a website for the first time and you're on a tight budget, then shared hosting is the best option as well.

Shared web hosting will usually cost between $3 - $15/month. Some web hosts will try to charge as much as $40/month for shared hosting, but that's too much money. WordPress is a very simple script, and it doesn't require that many resources to host a WordPress website.

On average, most people pay about $7/month for WordPress hosting annually. With a small investment of about $84, you can prepay your web hosting account for an entire year.

The only drawback to shared web hosting is that everybody on your designated server is "sharing" the resources. So if someone on your shared hosting account has a huge spike in website visitors, this could cause your website to load slower or act sluggish.

This generally isn't a problem because there are administrators watching the web servers 24/7. If someone is consistently sucking up all the resources on a shared hosting account, the hosting provider will contact the offender and make them upgrade to *VPS* or *Dedicated* hosting.

VPS Hosting

VPS stands for "virtual private server." VPS hosting takes a single server and divides it into 2 or more virtual web servers. Each virtual web server acts as if it's an independent machine, and it doesn't share resources.

Since you're not sharing resources or disk space, your website will run a lot faster. Your website is also more secure with *VPS hosting* compared to *shared web hosting*. With shared hosting, if a hacker gains access to one website on the server, then the hacker could cause problems for everybody sharing the same server.

With VPS hosting, everything is on you! You can install stronger security measures and you have full control over your virtual machine. There are several different packages for VPS hosting depending on how much disk space you need. The good thing about VPS hosting is that you can easily upgrade to more disk space without moving your website to a new server.

The drawback to VPS hosting is that you need to have some experience with web host administration. Your web host will give you access to the server to upload/download whatever software you want. If you don't know what you're doing, then you'll end up confused.

If you're new to web hosting, then this probably isn't a good option. If you really think you'll need a VPS because of the type of business you're starting, then you can always opt for a Managed VPS. A Managed VPS means that someone at the data center will manage the server for you to make sure everything is set up correctly based on your business.

VPS hosting can cost anywhere between **$30 - $150/month** depending on your needs. If you expect to receive large amounts of website visitors and you need to handle the traffic, then you should go with VPS hosting. If you don't have time to learn web hosting administration, then opt for the "Managed VPS" and you'll be fine.

Dedicated Server

A dedicated server is like a VPS except the machine isn't divided. With dedicated hosting, you receive an entire web server to yourself. Dedicated servers allow you to do anything you want; the entire server is yours. You're basically renting an entire machine from the web host, and they're just keeping it cool for you in there air conditioned data center.

This is the most expensive type of hosting. Huge websites like Facebook, Amazon, Pinterest, and all the other big names use dedicated servers. They actually use multiple dedicated servers because they can't afford to have their websites crash or go offline. Dedicated servers cost between $100 - $500/month.

Searching For WordPress Web Hosting

There are thousands of web hosting companies that can host a WordPress website. Before choosing a hosting provider, here are some of the most important features that you'll need to consider:

Disk Space

Disk space measures how much information you can store on the server. Most web hosts will give you a lot more disk space that you'll ever need. A basic WordPress website usually only has a few static pages like a contact page, about us page, terms and conditions page, sales page, and then a blog.

If you plan on creating a dynamic website that has a lot of videos, mp3 files, and photos, then you'll probably need 2 or 3 gigabytes (GB) of disk space. Usually the cheapest shared hosting plan comes with at least 10 gigabytes of disk space, so you'll still have more than enough space.

If you're still unsure how much disk space you'll require, don't worry about it. I'll refer you to a few WordPress hosts that offer **UNLIMITED** disk space for your WordPress website.

Bandwidth

Bandwidth is a measure of how much data is transferred to and from your hosting account. Some web hosts may refer to bandwidth as a "Transfer Limit" and it's measured in gigabytes. Your bandwidth is consumed anytime someone visits your website and clicks around visiting multiple pages.

Your bandwidth is also consumed when you upload photos, videos, WordPress themes, WordPress plugins, check your email, and so on. Most people never use up their disk space, but some people have been known to use up their bandwidth.

Your bandwidth limit is reset once per month, so you have to stay within your allotted bandwidth limits for about 30 days. If you go over your bandwidth limits, it'll be rather expensive to purchase more bandwidth. Once again, don't worry about it. I'll refer you to a few WordPress hosts the offer **UNLIMITED** bandwidth so you'll never go over the limit.

MySQL Databases

Databases are used to store information. Web programs called "Scripts" usually require a database to store information, and databases get accessed daily. Databases are important because WordPress will require at least one database to function on your web host.

20 – 30 databases should be more than enough because most NEW WordPress users only use 1 database. At the very most, I personally only use about 6 databases even though I have a hosting plan that offers unlimited databases. I'll refer you to a WordPress host that

offers **UNLIMITED** MySQL Databases if you want to play it safe.

My Top 3 Recommended WordPress Hosts

Based on the previous section, some of the most important features to consider when choosing a WordPress hosts are:

- **Disk Space** (at least several gigabytes)
- **Bandwidth** (the more, the better)
- **MySQL Databases** (a WordPress website requires at least 1 database)

With that in mind, you'll understand why I'm recommending the following WordPress hosts for new WordPress users.

1.) **Bluehost $6.95 - $7.95/month (#1 Recommended by Wordpress.org)**

Bluehost offers:

- cPanel
- Unlimited Domain Hosting (including Databases)
- Unlimited GB Hosting Space (Disk Space)
- Unlimited GB File Transfer (Bandwidth)
- Unlimited Email Accounts

- Free Domain Name (1st year only)
- 24/7 Phone, Chat, Email Support
- VPS Hosting
- Dedicated Hosting

Bluehost gives you unlimited everything, you'll get a free domain name, they have cPanel, and they have 24/7/365 customer support. Bluehost is also well established since 1996, and that's right around the time when the internet started to become popular. Bluehost is extremely easy to use, and that's one of the reasons why they are the #1 recommended web hosts by *WordPress.org*.

Bluehost used to only offer shared hosting, but they've recently started offering VPS and Dedicated hosting as well. Check out their website now for more details.

2.) **Go Daddy $2.99 - $7.49 (Current discounted prices)**

Go Daddy offers 3 different hosting packages for WordPress users. They have an *Economy* Package, *Deluxe* Package, and *Ultimate* Package.

Economy Plan $2.99/month

- 100 GB space
- Unlimited Bandwidth
- 100 email accounts
- 10 MySQL Databases

- HCC (Hosting Control Center)
- 24/7 Phone & Email Support
- Month-to-month hosting available

Do not choose the *Economy Plan*. Although they offer 10 MySQL databases, you can only host **one website** on that plan. If you decide to start a new website, you'll have to buy another hosting package for your new website.

Deluxe Plan $4.49/month

- Unlimited Space
- Unlimited Websites & Bandwidth
- 500 Email Accounts
- 25 MySQL Databases
- HCC (Hosting Control Center)
- 24/7 Phone & Email Support
- Month-to-month hosting available

The *Deluxe* plan gives you the best value for your money. This plan is similar to the hosting package offered by Bluehost. This plan is currently on sale for $4.49/month, but it's usually about $8/month just like Bluehost.

Ultimate Plan $7.49/month

- Unlimited Websites, Space, & Bandwidth
- Unlimited Email Accounts
- Unlimited MySQL Databases
- HCC (Hosting Control Center)
- Website Accelerator
- Free SSL Certificate (So you can securely accept credit cards online)
- 24/7 Phone & Email Support
- Month-to-month hosting available

If you decide to go with Go Daddy, then choose either the Deluxe or Ultimate Plan. Go Daddy also offers *VPS Hosting* and *Dedicated Hosting*.

As I mentioned earlier in this book; most shared hosting accounts usually costs in between $3 - $15 month, so prices are subject to change. If Go Daddy increases their price by the time you read this book, then can use the promo code: **WOW24720**. That promo code will discount 20% off your first purchase if you're a new Go Daddy customer.

If the promo code above doesn't work, just ask the customer service rep to find a promo code for you. Go Daddy is always offering some type of special promotion to save you money. Check out their website now for more details.

3.) **InMotion Hosting 5.99 - $13.99/month**

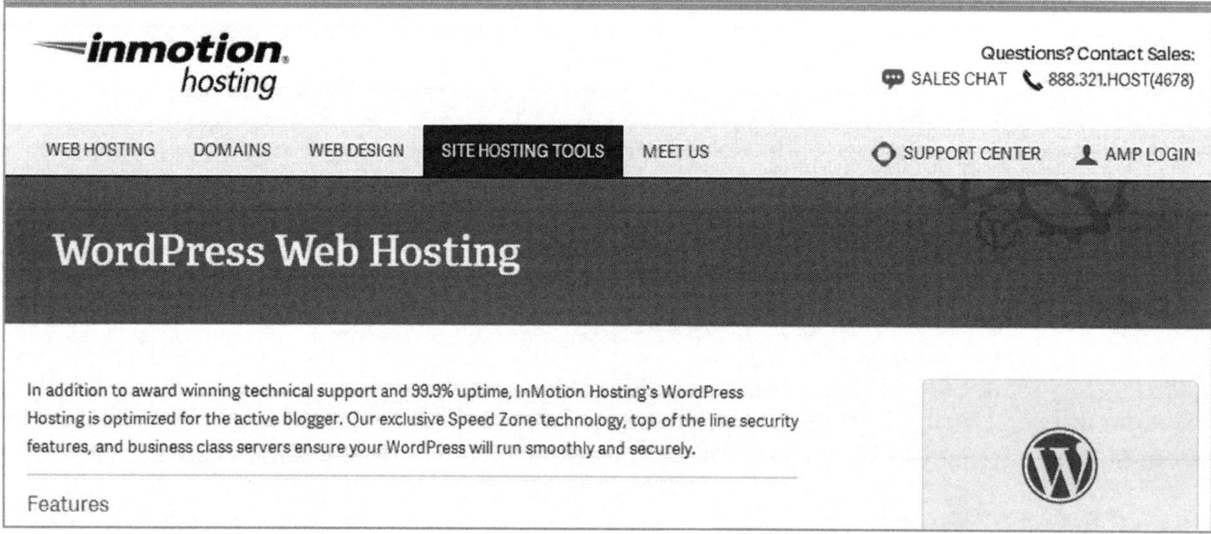

InMotion offers 3 different hosting packages just like Go Daddy. Their packages are called **Launch**, **Power**, and **PRO**. Just like Go Daddy, their introductory package won't allow you to create that many websites. If you decide to host with InMotion, choose the Power or Pro package. Here's a list of features:

- cPanel
- Unlimited Disk Space
- Unlimited GB File Transfer (Bandwidth)
- Spam Safe Email
- Data Backup every 24 hours
- Host up to 25 websites on one account
- Max Speed Zone Technology

The reason InMotion makes our list is because they offer **Speed Zone Technology**. InMotion allows you to choose the data center that hosts your website. So if you're on the east coast, you can choose a data center on the east coast and your website will perform faster. They also have a data center on the West Coast, so if you live on the west coast you can choose that data center.

If you live within InMotion's **Max Speed Zones**, your website will move lighting fast. You'll have to check their website to find out if you're within their max speed zones or not. This type of hosting is perfect if you have a local business. All your local customers will have a great user experience when viewing your website. The faster your website, the better!

InMotion offers special discounts weekly because they need to stay competitive just like everybody else. Check out InMotions website now for more details.

Do Your Own Research

The WordPress hosts I've recommended are **excellent** based on personal experience. You should always do your own research before deciding on a hosting provider.

There are thousands of web hosts, so it's impossible for anybody to try them all and call one particular host "the best." You should read reviews online about different web hosts, and then narrow down your selection to three hosting providers.

Make sure that you select a web host that specializes in WordPress and offers cPanel/Hosting Control Center. The best way to search for hosting providers is to use Google, Yahoo, and Bing. Search for the phrases:

1.) WordPress hosting

2.) cPanel hosting

3.) Best WordPress hosting providers

You can also visit **Wordpress.org** and you'll see a list of their top recommended WordPress hosting providers. After you do your own research, I guarantee that you'll see Bluehost, Go Daddy, and InMotion mentioned everywhere.

After you make a list of the top 3 web hosts that you're interested in; the next step is to call each host and ask them a lot of questions. In the next section, I'll cover some important questions that you'll need the answers too before you make your final decision.

What Type of Customer Support is Available?

Customer support is very important. My cousin decided to use a no-name budget hosting company to save about $60/year. She may have saved $60, but it took her almost two weeks to install WordPress on her hosting account.

The web host she used didn't have the "one-click install" feature for WordPress, and they didn't offer 24/7 **free** tech support to help her. She was only paying $1/month for web hosting, but was it really worth it? Every time she called the hosting company, there was a 50/50 chance if someone would pick up the phone or not. She eventually had to switch hosting companies so she wasted her time and money.

Before choosing a WordPress host, you need to find out what type of support they offer. For example, if you're having problems installing WordPress, will they help you install the software?

Does the web hosts offer 24/7 customer support? Your website will be available 24/7 so it makes sense to have 24/7 hosting support depending on your business. Some hosting providers offer 24/7 customer support, but if you call at 3 am, nobody is there to pick up the phone.

What type of customer support does the web host offer? Some web hosts will only offer email support and will take up to 24 hours to respond. Can your business wait 24 hours to get a problem handled? I know I can't wait 24 hours if something goes wrong with one of my websites. I need my problems fixed right away, so I need 24/7/365 phone support available at all times.

If your website goes down, are you patient enough to wait 24 hours for an email response? If the answer is "No" then you should choose a host that offers 24/7 phone support; or at least a reasonably short guaranteed response time by email.

Hosting Policies and Guarantees

I know a few people that wanted to start an *Adult* and/or *Gambling* website. Some web hosts **will not allow** these types of websites, so you should read the "Terms of Service" before you choose a web host. If you're still not sure, then call the web host to verify what type of content they allow.

For example, I know for a fact that Bluehost will not allow adult related websites at all. One of the reasons for this is that most shared hosting accounts are sharing the same IP address. So if someone on a shared hosting account uploads illegal porn, the IP address could get banned or black-listed and that can affect everybody on the server that's sharing the same IP address.

What about Money Back Guarantees?

Most WordPress hosts should offer a 30-day money back guarantee. If their web hosting service is "so amazing" then they should be happy to let you try their service for 30 days risk free.

You'll also need to find out how a potential web host handles prepaid accounts. For example, if you pay for a full year of hosting and you decide to cancel 2 months later; will the web host give you a pro-rated refund? Some hosts don't offer pro-rated refunds or any refunds at all. So make sure you ask about their refund policies before you purchase web hosting from anybody.

Special Offers

Some WordPress hosting providers offer free perks if you sign up with them. You need to always read the *terms and conditions* before you accept any special offers. Actually it's better to call the web host and ask them what the stipulations are to any "free" offers. Some common free offers include:

Free Domain Name

Some WordPress hosts will offer you a free domain name. 90% of the time the "free" domain name is only free for the first year. After the first year, you'll have to re-register the domain yourself which will cost between $8-$15/year depending on your domain registrar.

The price of a domain name varies depending on which web host you're using. Some web hosts will have a flat fee of $10/year for all domain names while other hosts will only charge you $2/year for a domain. The price difference usually depends on the domain name extension. For example, **.net**, **.info**, **.us**, and **.org** are usually less expensive than a **.com** domain name.

Web hosts usually give you a free domain name when you sign up for a 1 year prepaid hosting account. If you decide to leave the web hosts within the first year, they may not release your domain name and keep it. That will cause a major problem if you've spent a lot of time promoting that domain name.

If you're not sure if you'll stay with a web host for at least a year, then you should register your own domain and decline to use the free domain. You can purchase your domain name separately from a domain registrar like NameCheap or Go Daddy.

Free SSL Certificates

SSL certificates encrypt your website so you can securely accept credit cards. Free SSL certificate promotions usually work the same way as free domain promotions. The SSL is free for the first year and then you'll have to re-register the following year at your own expense.

You should find out how much the SSL certificate costs to make sure you can afford it. Depending on how you set up your payments with the web host, they might automatically charge your debit card to re-register the SSL certificate after it expires.

A basic SSL certificate can cost anywhere from **$60 - $100/year**. Depending on your financial situation, an unexpected charge on your debit card for $60 - $100 might cause a problem. If you really need the SSL certificate, keep close track of the expiration date so you're ready to renew it after the free period expires.

Referral Programs

Some web hosts will offer you special discounts, referral fees, or even free hosting if you refer your friends to them. If you find a web host that you like, find out if they offer a referral program. With some web hosts, you'll only need to refer about 3 people per year to cover your web hosting fees for the year.

Once again, make sure you ask plenty of questions before you decide on a WordPress hosting provider. The most important feature is always customer support for new website owners. As a new webmaster, you'll probably need to call customer support a lot in the beginning to help you troubleshoot minor issues.

You should now have an idea of what to look for when choosing a WordPress hosting provider. Narrow your list down to at least 3 choices and choose the best one based on your needs. In the next chapter I'll give you an overview of *cPanel* and your *Hosting Control Center.*

Chapter 2

Welcome to cPanel

After you purchase a web hosting account; your web host will send you an email with your username and password for cPanel. Make sure that you save that email into a special folder or print the email out and save it.

If you never received the email, then make sure to check your spam folder. If you still can't find the email with your account information, then contact your web hosts over the phone.

The next step is to sign onto cPanel using your username and password. If you don't have a web hosting account yet, you can log into an **online demo** account and still follow along with me.

Here's a link to log into a demo cPanel account for Bluehost:

- **http://read2learn.net/DEMO**

Click the link on the page that says "online demo site." *See Figure 1.*

Figure 1

Even though I'm going to use Bluehost in the following examples; your cPanel will you look **very similar** to the "Bluehost Online Demo." Keep in mind that cPanel is a 3rd party software that most web hosts install to make website management easier.

It doesn't matter if you're hosting with Bluehost, InMotion, or Hostgator; your cPanel interface will have the same commonly used features. Here's a glimpse of what cPanel looks like:

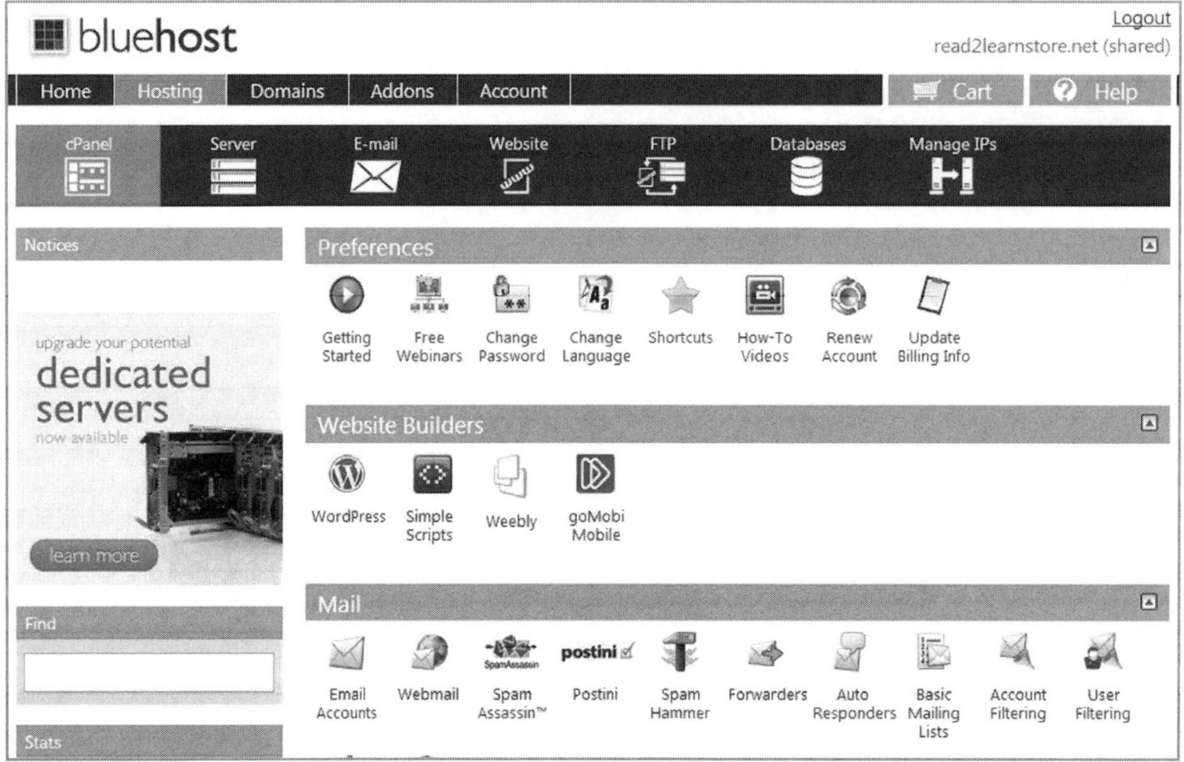

cPanel offers different themes, so your cPanel screen might look different. Your web host might also offer different features which I'll discuss later. At first glance, this screen may looks confusing but it's not.

Starting at the top right of the screen, you have a basic "log out" button. Always make sure to log out when you're finish using cPanel. Directly below the "log out" link, you'll see your website address along with the type of hosting that's associated with your domain name.

Below that section you'll see a menu that says **Home**, **Hosting**, **Domains**, **Addons**, and **Account**. Those are just <u>shortcuts</u> that you can use later once you get familiar with cPanel.

Below that menu, you see another menu that says **cPanel** (the current screen you're on), **Server**, **Email**, **Website**, **FTP**, **Databases**, and **Manage IP's**. Once again, those are <u>shortcuts</u> to the most important cPanel features. A lot of these top menus have links that'll forward you to the exact same pages, so don't become overwhelmed with this screen.

After I explain some of the commonly used cPanel features; I'll refer back to the top menus and you'll notice that they lead to the same places. Before I start discussing the different cPanel options, I want to direct your attention to the "**Stats**" section on the left side of the screen.* (See Figure 2.)

**You'll only see "Stats" if you're logged into an active cPanel. You won't see any stats if you're logged into a demo cPanel account.*

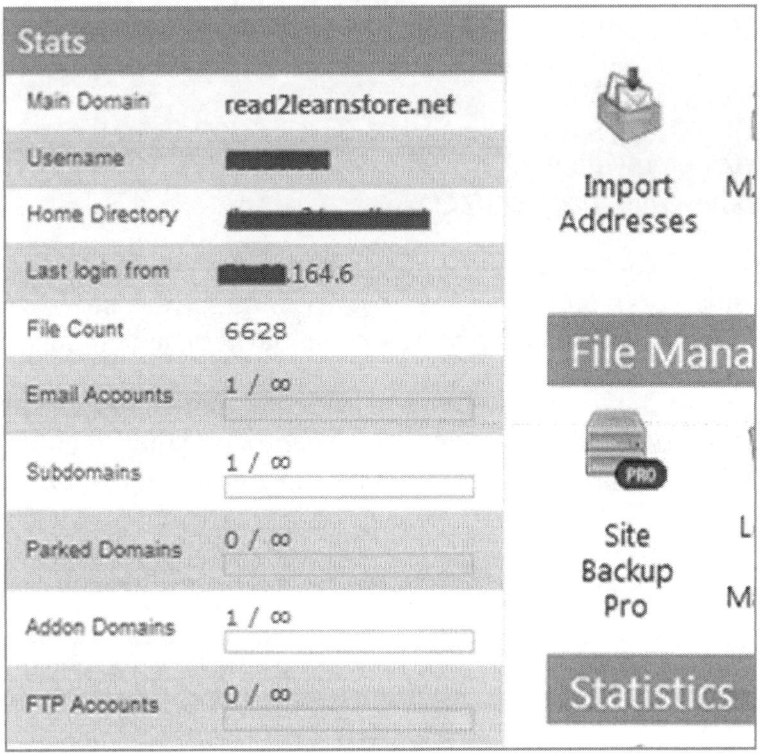

Figure 2

Main Domain: This is the main domain you chose when you opened your hosting account.

Username: cPanel username, but you can also log in using your website address.

Home Directory: Directory where your website files are stored.

Last Login From: This shows the IP address of the last person that logged into your cPanel. You should pay close attention to this IP address. If you only log into cPanel from your home office, then your IP address should be the same every time you log in.

File Count: How many files you have.

Email Accounts: This shows you how many email accounts you've created versus how many you're allowed to have. I've only created one email account, and Bluehost offers unlimited emails. If you look at *Figure 2*, it shows "1/infinite symbol" next to the email accounts section.

Subdomains: This section will show you how many sub-domains you have versus how many you're allowed to have. Bluehost offers unlimited sub-domains, so once again you'll notice the "infinite symbol" in that section.

Sub-domains are prefixed to the main domain. Sub-domains are used to make certain parts of your website easier to find. For example, the sub-domain maps.google.com takes you directly to Google Maps.

If I were to make training videos on my website, I could create an easy to remember sub-domain like videos.bestwebhostinginc.com.

Parked Domains: Parked domains are other domains that you own that are currently pointing to your main domain. For example, I could purchase *bestwebhostinginc.org*, *bestwebhostinginc.info*, and *webhostinghelp.com* and park those domains.

If someone were to visit those parked domains, the domain will mirror the same content on my main website at *bestwebhostinginc.com*. This section on your cPanel will show you how many parked domains you have versus the maximum amount allowed.

Add-on Domains: Add-on domains are similar to parked domains. The main difference is that add-on domains get treated as if they were a completely different website.

If you noticed, the main domain for our Bluehost account is *read2learnstore.net*. Kent Mauresmo (the other author of this book) created an Add-on domain for me which is *bestwebhostinginc.com*.

This item on your cPanel will show you how many add-on domains you've created versus how many you're allowed to have. Since Bluehost allows unlimited add-on domains, you can create multiple WordPress websites with different content.

FTP Accounts: FTP stands for File Transfer Protocol. People use FTP accounts to transfer files from their personal computer to their web server. Since you're using WordPress, you probably won't use FTP accounts that often.

Your WordPress dashboard does *almost* everything that an FTP account does. For example, most people use FTP accounts to upload web pages, images, or their entire website.

If you're familiar with WordPress, then you know that you can upload images, themes, plugins, and new pages by using your WordPress dashboard. WordPress already has an built in FTP.

There may be a few situations when need to use an FTP account. For example, you might have trouble uploading a theme through your WordPress dashboard because the file is too large. In a situation like this, you can upload the theme using a FTP client like Filezilla. I'll talk more about FTP later, but this item will show you how many FTP accounts you've created versus how many you have available.

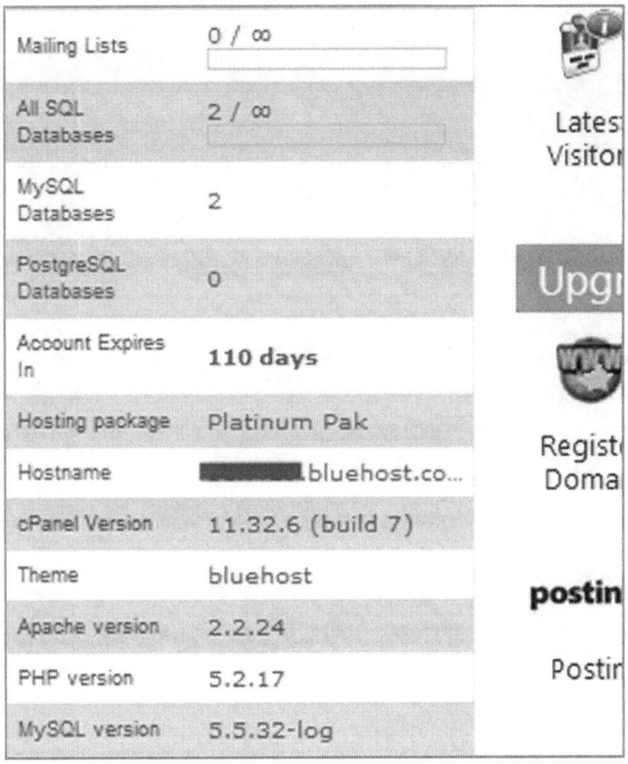

Mailing Lists	0 / ∞
All SQL Databases	2 / ∞
MySQL Databases	2
PostgreSQL Databases	0
Account Expires In	**110 days**
Hosting package	Platinum Pak
Hostname	.bluehost.co...
cPanel Version	11.32.6 (build 7)
Theme	bluehost
Apache version	2.2.24
PHP version	5.2.17
MySQL version	5.5.32-log

Mailing Lists: This shows the current number of mailing lists you've created versus the total number allowed. cPanel includes mailing lists software that'll allow you to send out newsletters and updates. I'll give you more information about this feature later.

All SQL Databases: This item shows you the total number of databases (MySQL & PostgreSQL) you're using versus the total number allowed. A WordPress website will require at least one MySQL Database to work properly.

MySQL Databases: The section will show you how many MySQL Databases you're using.

PostgreSQL Databases: This section shows you how many PostgreSQL databases you're using. WordPress doesn't require this type of database to function.

Account Expires In: Here you'll see how many days you have left until your hosting account expires. You'll also receive an email when your hosting account is close to expiring as well.

Hosting Package: This shows you which hosting plan you're on. For example, Go Daddy offers 3 different packages:

- Economy (basic)
- Deluxe (best value)
- Ultimate (PRO package)

Hostname: Web host name for the purpose of mapping the hostname to an address, or the reverse process. You won't need to worry about this for the most part.

cPanel Version: This section shows you which version of cPanel you're using. There's a 90% chance you'll be using the most current version of cPanel depending on your web host.

Theme: This item tells you which theme you're using for cPanel. cPanel has multiple themes which is why your cPanel interface may look somewhat different. The screenshots I'm using are from the "Bluehost Theme."

Apache Version: This is the version of the web page serving software that is running.

PHP Version: This is the version of the PHP programming language that is currently installed on the server. Make sure that you choose a web hosts that has the most current version of PHP installed. Some WordPress themes and plugins require the latest version of PHP to work correctly.

MySQL version: This section will show you which version of MySQL is currently installed on the server.

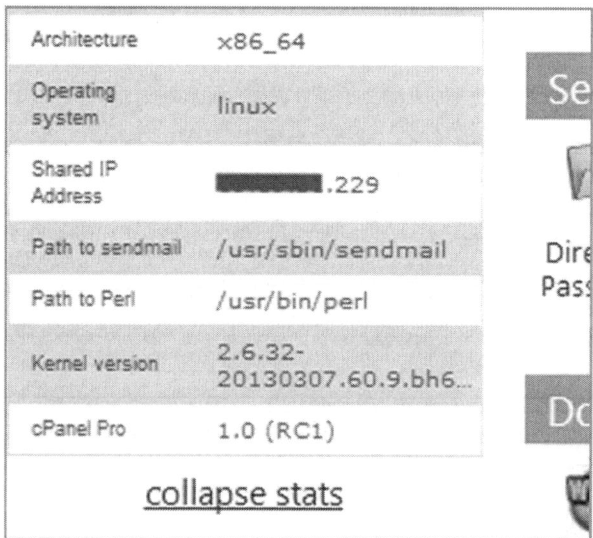

Architecture: This is the architecture of your server. An output of **x86_64** means you use a 64-bit server.

Operating System: The operating system that your server is running. There's a 90% chance this will be *Linux* unless you have a dedicated server and you're running Windows.

Shared IP Address: This is the IP address that your website and cPanel account are on. This IP address is shared with other web hosting accounts on the same server. You can also purchase a dedicated IP address that's only assigned to your domain name. The only time you'll need to purchase a dedicated IP address is if you want an SSL certificate for your website.

Path to Sendmail: This is where the process that handles sending mail is.

Path to Perl: This is the path to Perl on your server.

Kernel Version: Kernel is the core of the Linux operating system. This section shows you which version you're using.

cPanel Pro: cPanel Pro allows developers to add new features to Cpanel. You don't have to worry about this section because you're new to cPanel.

Go Daddy Users

If you're using Go Daddy's hosting control center, your stats section will look a little bit different. Follow these steps to launch Go Daddy's hosting control center:

- Log into your Go Daddy account, and then click "My Account."

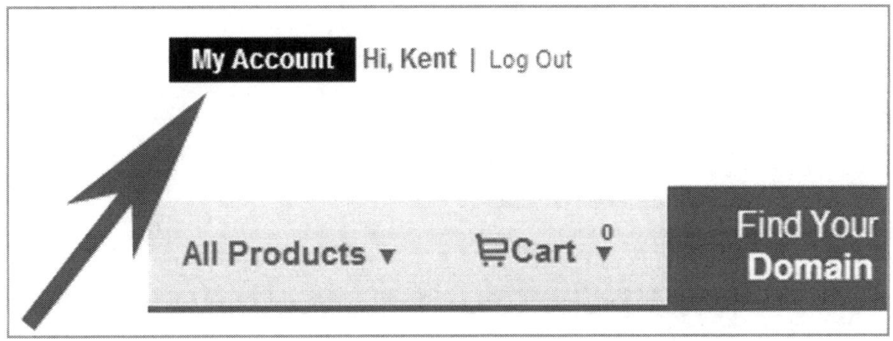

- Click the "Launch" button in the "Web Hosting" row.

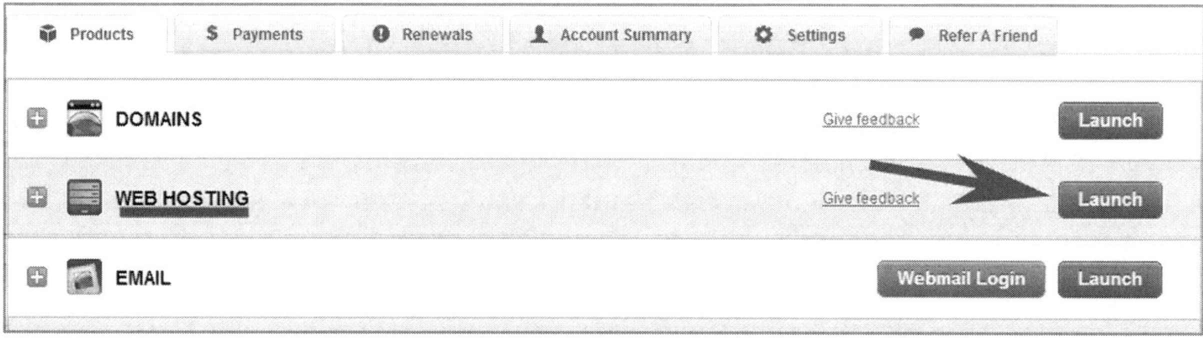

On the right side of the screen, you'll see your "Account Snapshot."

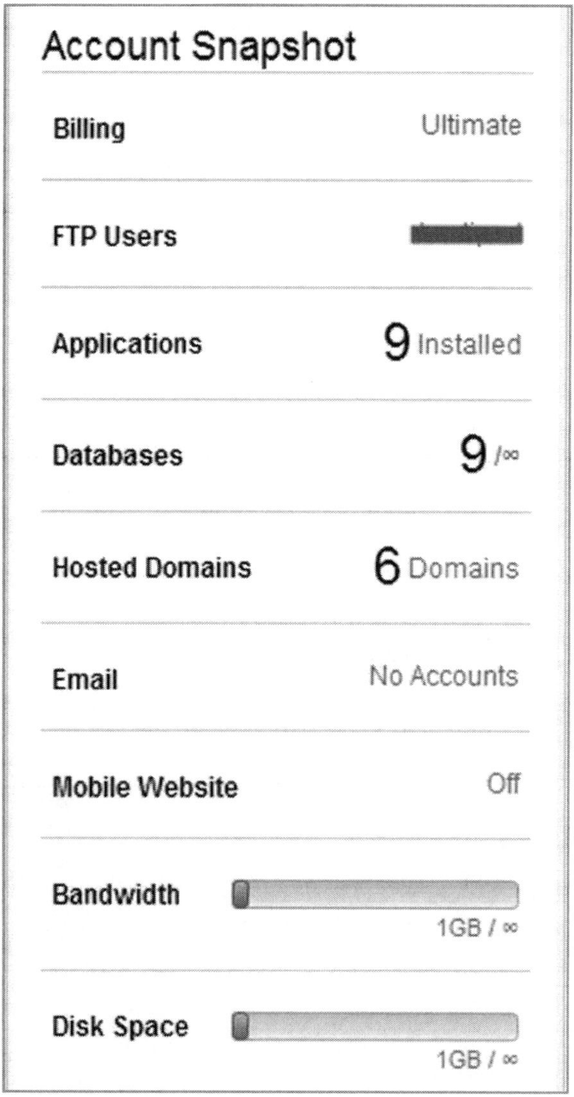

Below the account snapshot, you'll see a section that has your "Server Details." Click the "details" link to expand the list.

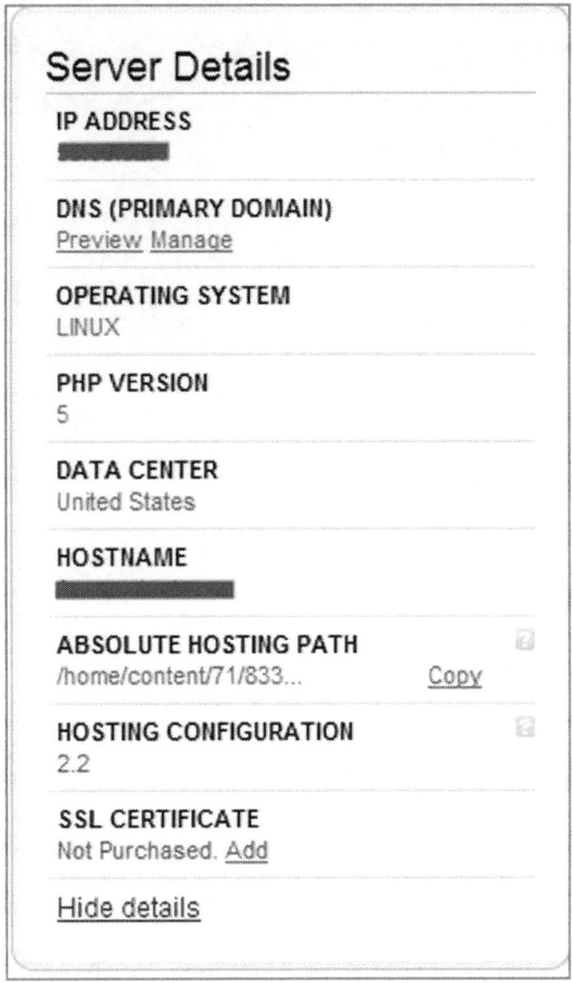

Some of the information displayed on the stats section in cPanel isn't displayed on Go Daddy's "hosting control center" screen. Don't be alarmed. As you progress through this book, you'll notice that both cPanel and Go Daddy's Hosting Control Center offer the same information, just on different screens.

That's pretty much it for the stats section! The next time you log into cPanel, you can look at your stats with **confidence** and you'll understand what you're looking at.

In the next chapter I'm going to log into the "Bluehost Demo" version of cPanel. I'll go over the "icons" within each section to help you easily understand what's happening within your control panel.

Chapter 3

cPanel Partners & Preferences

If you haven't already done so, log into the Bluehost Online Demo. Even if you're currently hosting your website with a different web host; you should be able to easily follow along.

Each web host has the option to customize, add and remove features from cPanel. If you're not hosting with Bluehost then your cPanel may look slightly different; but the most important features will still be there.

You'll notice a lot of "icons" on your main cPanel interface. In this chapter I'm going to discuss the first two rows of icons:

- **Partners**
- **Preferences**

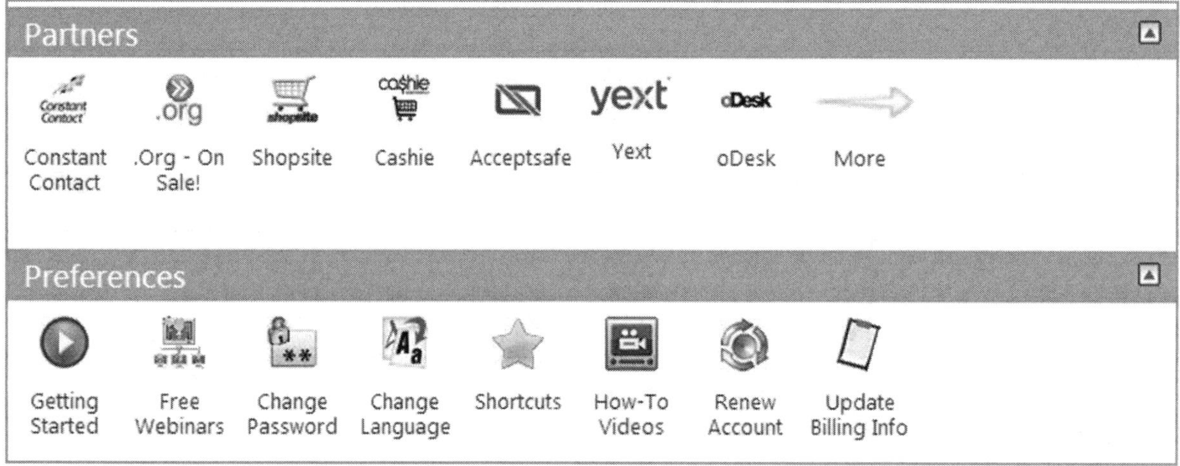

Partners

The "partners" section is exactly what it sounds like. Within this section you'll see a few partners and affiliates of the web host. This section is full of promotional products, and this is the web hosts way of making a few extra dollars.

The items within the "partners" section will be different depending on your web host. For example, Bluehost has teamed up with *Constant Contact*, *Cashie*, *Accept Safe*, *Yext*, and a few other companies that may offer services that you're interested in.

You'll also notice that Bluehost has an icon that says, "**.Org – On Sale!**" If you click that icon you'll get forwarded to a page that'll prompt you to buy another domain name. If you click the "More" arrow, you'll get forwarded to a section that displays even more partner sites such as "Google Adwords" which is an advertising platform for Google.

This entire section is just paid "add-ons" that you probably won't need. If you think you might need some of these promotional services, you can always come back to this section later.

I think the "partners" section adds extra clutter to your cPanel. The "partners" section makes your cPanel look way more confusing than it has to be, and I think that it's wasting space.

If you agree with me, than you have the option to "collapse" this section (or any other section.) You can also "drag and drop" this section to the bottom of the screen if you want to completely get it out the way.

To collapse this section, just click the arrow on the top right corner of the box. (*Figure 3.*)

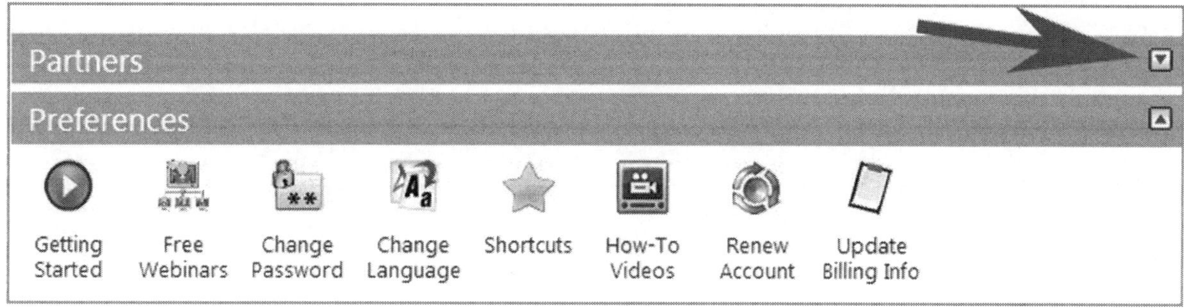

Figure 3

Preferences

The preferences section has some useful tools that you'll probably use. The very first item that you'll see is the "Getting Started" icon.

Getting Started

I don't think the "getting started" icon will help you *that* much. If you click the "getting started" icon, you'll get prompted to learn how to:

- Transfer your Domain Name
- Purchase a New Domain
- Assign Additional Domains to your Account

- Access Your Email
- Create an Email Account

You'll also learn how to access your email account using different platforms such as:

- Outlook 2010
- Outlook 2013
- Mail
- Thunderbird
- Outlook 2011
- iOS (iPhone, iPod Touch & iPad)
- Android

If you're just getting started, I think the "getting started" section is leaving out a lot of crucial information. I'll show you how to set up a professional email account later in this book. If you decide that you want to link your email account to *Microsoft Outlook*, *iPhone*, *Android*, or *Thunderbird*; then you can come back to this "Getting Started" section later to learn how.

Free Webinars

If you click the "free webinars" icon, you'll get forwarded to a screen that has a date for the next training webinar. You can sign up using your email address, and you'll receive reminders via email so you don't miss the webinar.

Change Password

Click this icon to change your cPanel password. You'll have to know your current password to create a new password. You can also use this section to create a separate password for your billing.

I don't recommend creating too many passwords because you'll probably get confused. Just make sure that your main password is "strong" and you shouldn't have any problems.

This section will also give you some tips to help you choose a strong password that's hard to break. You'll also learn a few other tips to help you protect your password and keep your cPanel account secure.

Change Language

This function allows you to change the language displayed in your cPanel interface. If you need a language that's not available, contact your web host and they'll install it for you.

Shortcuts

cPanel shortcuts are links that you can add to your desktop or your browser's toolbar. The shortcuts will allow you to access your cPanel account a lot easier.

You'll be provided with two links that you can drag to your desktop. One link will allow you to access cPanel from your desktop. The other link will allow you to access your webmail (email) from your desktop.

How to Videos

There are currently 42 "How-to" videos in this section. The videos are organized from "most viewed" to "least viewed." If you don't see a video for your specific problem, you can use the search feature on the top right of the screen.

There's also a dropdown menu to help you sort through the videos. You can sort the videos by:

- Relevance
- Most Recent
- Most Viewed
- Most Helpful
- Most Solutions
- Resource Type

Renew Account

Click this icon to renew your hosting account. If your domain name is registered with another registrar (i.e. Go Daddy), make sure that you renew your domain name with that company to prevent downtime.

Update Billing Info

Click this icon to update your contact information, billing information, and your phone number. You can also decide if you want to receive promotional emails on this page.

That covers everything within the *Partners & Preferences* section. Feel free to "collapse" both of those rows so you can feel yourself moving forward.

Go Daddy

If you're using **Go Daddy's Hosting Control Center**, you'll find similar tools. Go Daddy has tabs to help you set up your preferences change passwords, manually renew your accounts, and a section to update your billing info.

Go Daddy also has extensive support tools if you need help with a specific problem. If the support tools aren't giving you the information you need, you can always call Go Daddy's 24/7 phone support. You can set up your preferences by clicking the tabs shown in *Figure 4*.

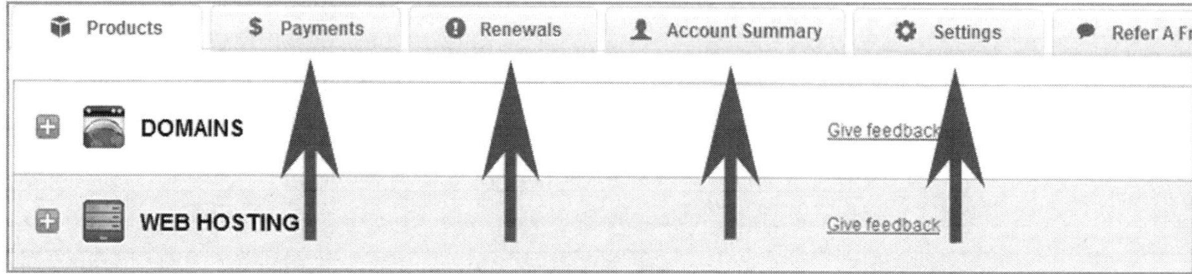

Figure 4

Payments: The payments tab allows you to add/delete credit cards.

Renewals: The renewals tab allows you to manually renew domains and hosting accounts.

Account Summary: The account summary tab shows you a list of all your recent orders and active products.

Settings: The settings tab allows you to update your personal information, change passwords, contact preferences, and a lot more.

If you need help or tech support with your hosting account, then click the "Support" button that's on the top right of your screen.

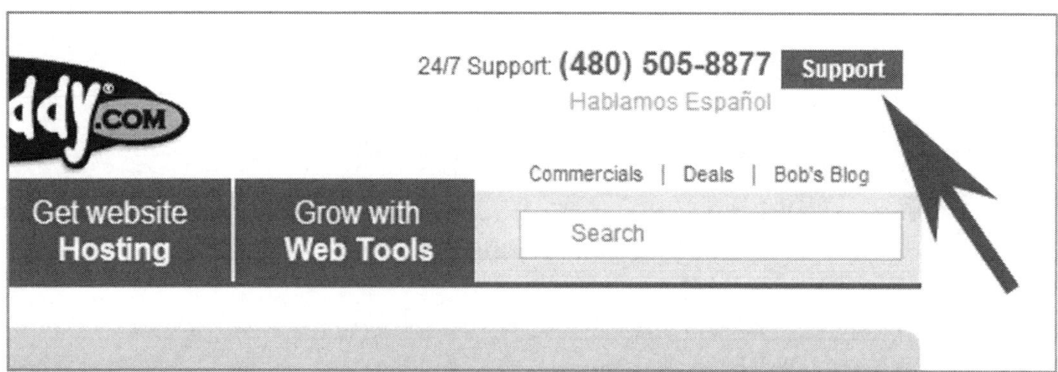

You'll get forwarded to another screen that offers product support for **Account Management**, **Domain Management**, **Go Daddy Email**, **Web Hosting**, **Website Builder**, and **All Products**. Just click the "plus symbol" to expand the menu and you'll find related help articles. (Figure 5.)

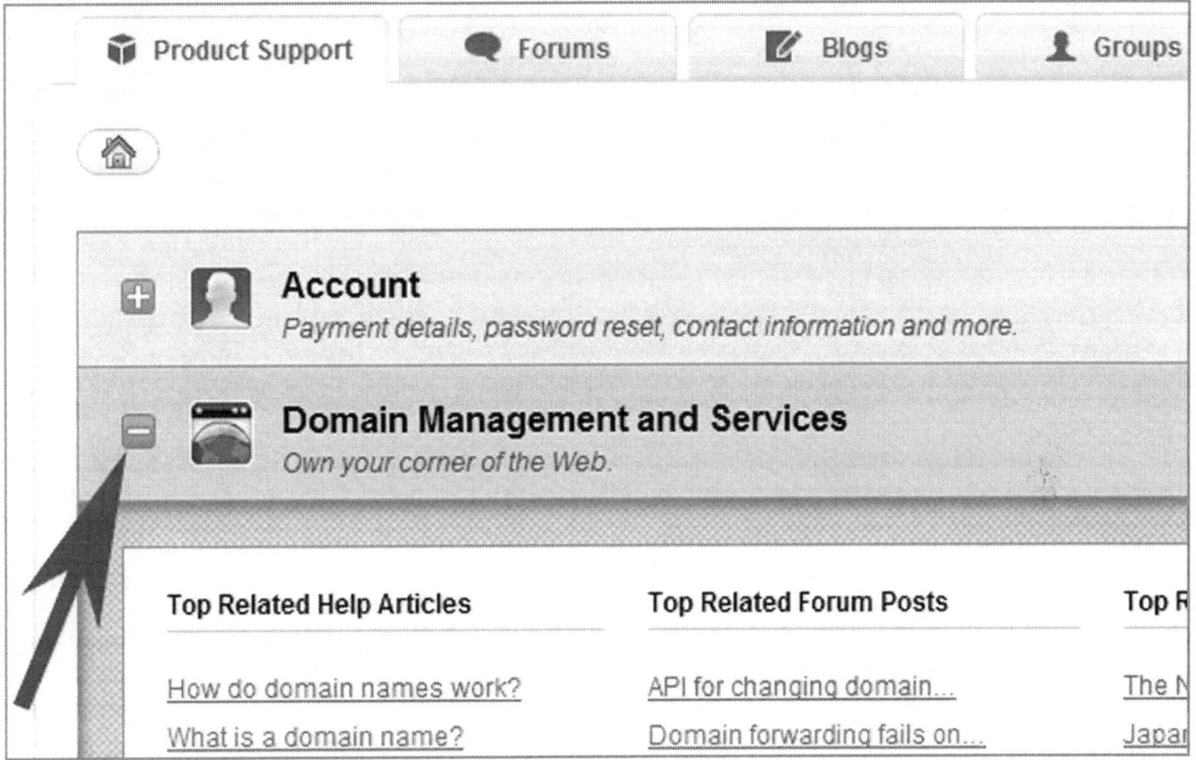

Figure 5

In the next chapter I'll show how to create new email accounts, access your email, set up forwards, and a lot more. I'll show you how to create email accounts using both **cPanel** and **HCC** (Hosting Control Center.)

Chapter 4

Email

You probably already have an email address at Yahoo, Gmail, or Hotmail, so you're probably wondering why you need to bother with another email address. If you're a business owner, then you want to be perceived as a **professional** company and not someone working out of their kitchen.

My partners and I get handed business cards all the time. The first thing we usually look at is the email address. If the person is using a Gmail account, then it's hard to take them serious. There's nothing wrong with Gmail, but it'll make people wonder if you're a *real* business or not.

I'll show you how to **easily** set up an email address attached to your domain name. It's important to note that you shouldn't abandon your free email account with Gmail, Yahoo, etc. You need to have at least one backup email with the free providers as well.

If you're ready, then log into your cPanel. If you don't have a hosting account set up yet, then log into the Bluehost online demo. Look for the "Mail" section which should look similar to the image below:

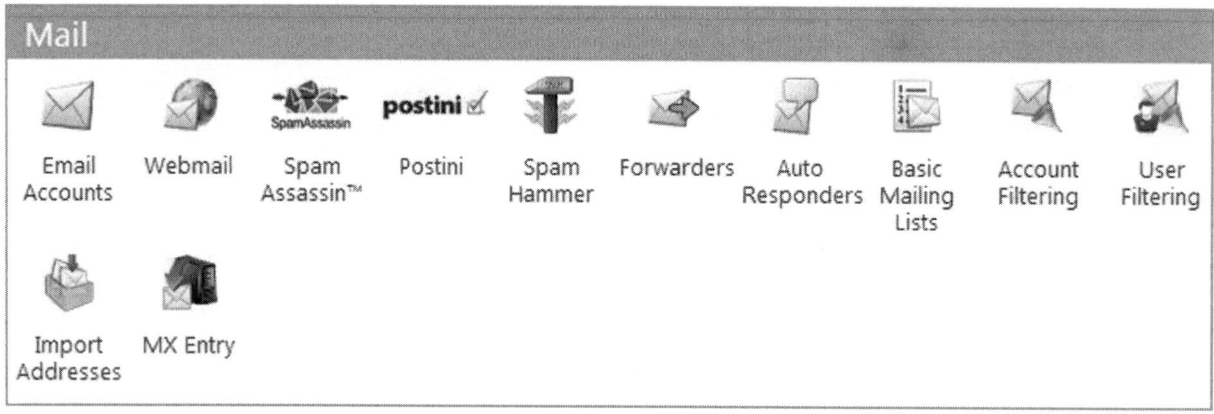

The very first icon says "Email Accounts." Click that icon to create an email account associated with your domain name. You'll have the option to choose your own password or have a strong password generated for you.

You can also set up your mail box quota on this page. By default your mail box quota is set to 250 MB, but you can change it to unlimited. You're only limited by the disk space permitted in your hosting plan. After you've set the quota, just click the "Create Account" button to create your new email address.

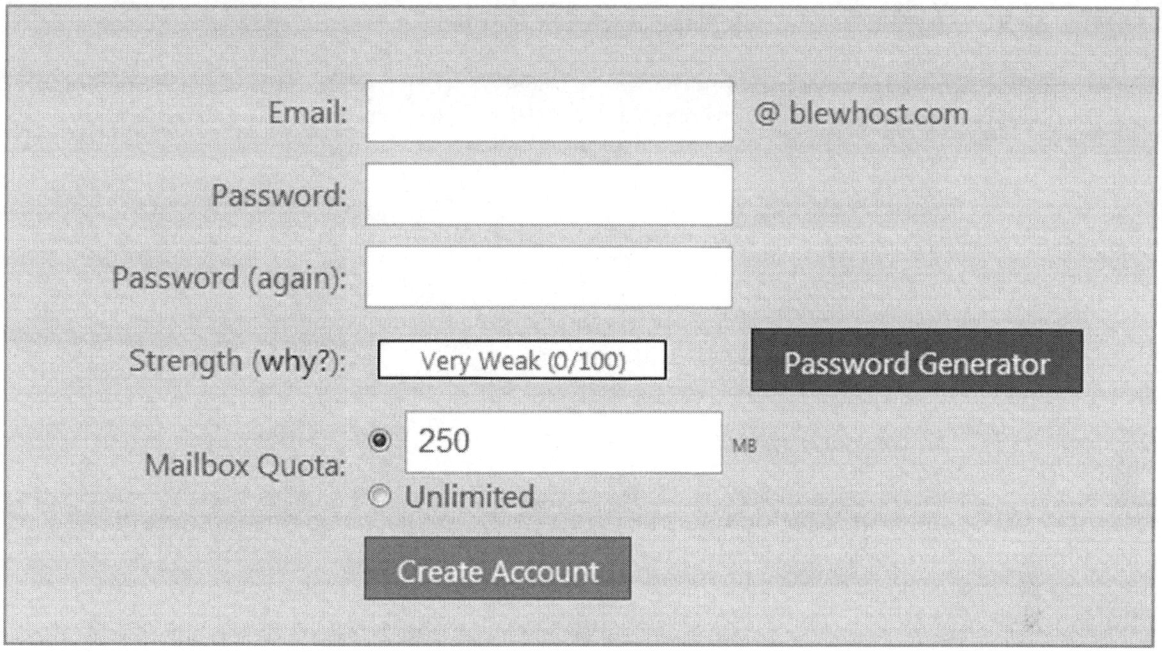

Email: [ ] @ blewhost.com
Password: [ ]
Password (again): [ ]
Strength (why?): Very Weak (0/100) Password Generator
Mailbox Quota: 250 MB / Unlimited
Create Account

Now that your account is created, I'm going to show you how to access your email account. Within the mail section of cPanel, click the icon that says "Webmail."

cPanel will forward you to a screen that'll prompt you to enter the email address and password that you're trying to access.

If you want to access your email directly without logging into cPanel, just type your domain name in your web browser followed by "**/webmail**." (Ex: *YourDomainName.com/webmail*) Once again, you'll be forwarded to the same screen prompting you to enter your email address and password.

After you enter your email address and password, you'll have the option to read your email from at least 3 different mail clients:

- Horde
- Roundcube
- SquirrelMail

I personally like the way the "Roundcube" interface looks. Click on each mail client and decide which one works best for you.

On the same screen where you choose your mail client, you'll notice a few icons below:

- **Change Password**: Change your email password.
- **Auto Responders**: You can set up an auto responder here. An example of an auto responder would read like, "Thank you for contacting us. We'll respond to your email within the next 24 hours."
- **Configure Mail Client**: This item will give you important information to help you sync your email with your Smartphone and/or Microsoft Outlook.
- **Email Filtering**: Set up filters to block certain emails based on your criteria.
- **Email Trace**: This tool displays a map showing you the mail server to which the email is delivered. This will help you diagnose problems sending email to a certain email address. You probably won't use this feature unless you're tech savvy. If you're having trouble sending/receiving emails, then just contact your web hosting provider.

You can log out of this "mail client" by clicking the *log out* link on the bottom right hand corner. Now let's go back to your cPanel dashboard and look at the other mail features available to you.

Spam Assassin

The next item within your mail section is *Spam Assassin*. Spam Assassin is an automated email filtering system that attempts to identify spam messages based on the content of the email's headers and body.

Click the "Spam Assassin" icon and you'll be taken to a screen where you'll have the option to enable this free program. You also have the option to set up a filter to auto delete spam messages. This filter will automatically delete messaged considered to be spam based on a score of 1–10.

You can also enable *Spam Box* on this screen. Spam Box will deliver any emails identified as SPAM by Spam Assassin into a separate mail folder named "spam". This "spam" folder will fill up and should be emptied regularly.

Postini

The next item you'll see is Postini. Postini is similar to Spam Assassin except that it's a paid service. *Postini Email Security* ensures your email is free from threats and junk mail, keeping your computers safe and productive. It blocks spam, viruses, phishing, and email threats.

Spam Hammer

The next item is Spam Hammer. *Spam Hammer* is a method of defending e-mail users against spam by "temporarily rejecting" any email from a sender it does not recognize.

If the mail is legitimate, the originating server will, after a delay, try again and if sufficient time has elapsed, the email will be accepted. Spam Hammer can only be enabled for a domain if it has email accounts.

cPanel offers you plenty of tools to stop SPAM. The absolute **easiest** way to avoid SPAM is to avoid entering your email address into any online forms. Use an alternate email address (Gmail, Yahoo, MSN) for online forms.

I rarely have problems with automated spam, and I've had my webmail address for over four years. I only get a few SPAM messages per week, and I just manually delete it myself. Be careful how you use SPAM software because they'll delete legitimate emails.

Forwarders

Forwarders allow you to send a copy of all mail from one email address to another. For example if you have two different email accounts, *matt123@example.com* and *matthew@example.com*; you could have your mail at *matt123@example.com* automatically forwarded to *matthew@example.com* so that you do not need to check both email accounts.

Keep in mind that the *forwarded email* will still be delivered to the original email address as well. This is a useful feature if you already your Gmail account synced with your Smart-phone. You can use the forwarding feature to forward your webmail to your Gmail account.

Just click the button that says *Add Forwarder* to begin. Enter the email address you want to forward along with the destination email address. Click the *Add Forwarder* button again to confirm.

You can also use forwarders to forward **all** emails from one domain to another. This will save you time compared to forwarding individual mail accounts. This feature is useful if you need to keep track of multiple webmail accounts.

Auto Responders

The next item says Auto Responders. If you recall earlier, we saw this same item on the webmail management screen. You can use auto responders to automatically send an email back to anyone who sends an email to a specified account. This can be useful if you're on vacation, unavailable, or if you have a generic message that you wish to send from a customer support email address.

Click the "Add Auto Responder" button to get started. There you'll find detailed instructions showing you how to set up the auto responder. For the most part, you probably won't need to use this feature even if you're on vacation. With all the Smart-phone's and tablets on the market, you can easily access your email 24/7 no matter where you're at.

Basic Mailing List

The next item within the mail section is for setting up a **basic** mailing list. If you need to send newsletters to small group of people, then you can use the basic mailing list feature within cPanel. This is a simple solution if you need to send out a newsletter to less than 100 people.

To create a list you have to click the "Basic Mailing List" icon. On the next screen you'll have to name your list, enter a password for the list, and click the button that says "Add Mailing List." You can configure specific settings for your list by clicking the "Modify" link.

If you have a mailing list larger than 100 users, then you can use another free program called *DadaMail*. You'll see a link to their website within cPanel. If you need something more advanced with multiple features, then you can use a paid solution called **Aweber**.

Account Filtering

Next on the list is the email filtering option. In this area you can manage filters for your main account. If you recall earlier, this option was also available on the webmail management screen. Filters are used to block e-mail based on your criteria.

You shouldn't have to use this feature for the most part. If you're receiving a lot of SPAM messages, just enable *Spam Assassin*.

User Filtering

The next item on your cPanel will say User Filtering. The difference between "Account Filtering" and "User Filtering" is simple. The account filtering option is for your main email account. The user filtering option is used to manage filters for each individual user.

If you want to set up filters for multiple email accounts, then use the "User Filter" option. Once again, you probably won't need to use this feature. Just enable *Spam Assassin* and that software will filter out most of the SPAM for you.

Import Addresses

The "import addresses" feature helps you **save time** if you need to set up a large number of email addresses/email forwarders. You may use Excel spreadsheet files (.xls) or comma-separated values sheet, aka CSV file (.csv) to import the data.

To import a list, click the "Import Addresses" icon on cPanel. Next, select which type of list you're trying to import; E-mail Accounts or Forwarders. Click the "Choose File" button to locate the file on your computer and upload the list. If you need help then visit the support area or contact your web host.

MX Entry

The final item within the mail section is an icon that says MX Entry. If you click that icon, you'll get redirected to a page that says "DNS Zone Editor." DNS stand for **Domain Name Servers.**

Zone files allow you to control how DNS functions. For example, if you need a domain or sub-domain to point to another IP address, use an A record. This is an advanced feature that you shouldn't play around with unless you're familiar with how DNS zones work.

If you're hosting a simple WordPress website, you probably won't ever use this feature. If the situation arises when you have to edit your DNS zone, just contact your web host and ask *tech support* to handle this for you.

Go Daddy Mail (Hosting Control Center)

I believe the webmail process for Go Daddy is more **simplified** compared to cPanel. Go Daddy doesn't come with unlimited free email accounts, but you'll get at least one free email account.

To get started with your Go Daddy webmail; log into your account and click the link that says "My Account" on the top left. You'll arrive at your hosting control center and you'll see the "Email" row. On that row you'll see a green button that says "Launch." Click the "launch" button.

Webmail Control Panel Menus

At the very top of the screen, you'll see a tab that says Domains, Hosting, and Email. You're currently on the *Email* tab, and the other tabs are shortcuts to the *Hosting* and *Domain* screens. I didn't mention these tabs earlier because I didn't want to confuse you. But the more you get comfortable with your web hosting account; you'll notice that there are shortcuts everywhere. (*Figure 6.*)

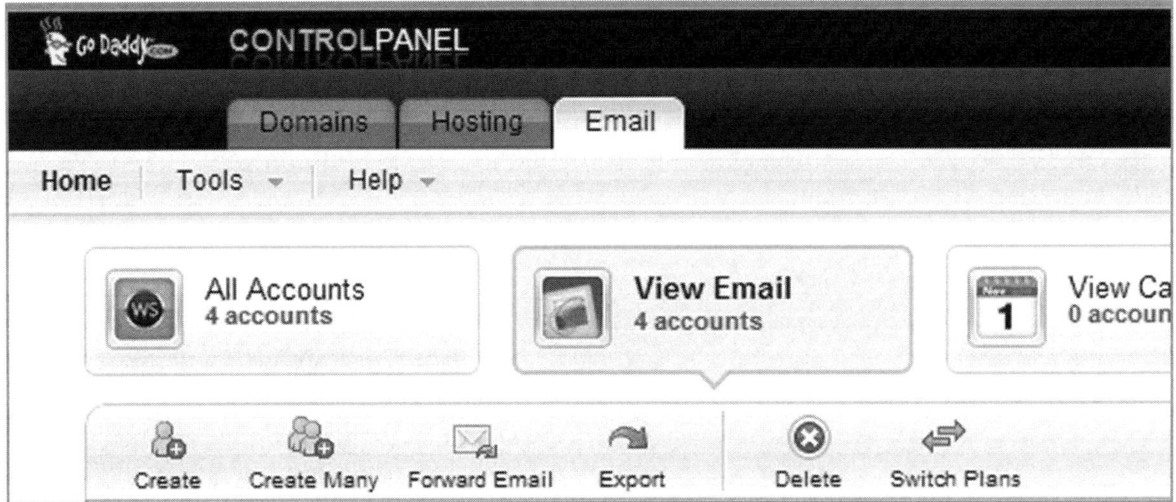

Figure 6

Under those tabs you'll see a menu that says **Home**, **Tools**, and **Help**. The "Home" link will navigate you to your email home page. The email home page will look like the same page you're currently on except with fewer options.

The next menu item says **"Tools."** The *tools* item will allow you to:

- View all your current email plans
- Customize your email login screen with your logo
- View your server settings. This is useful information if you plan to sync your email with your phone or Microsoft Outlook
- Download *Workspace Tools*. This program allows you to access your email directly from your desktop along with some other features
- Auto-Configure Microsoft Outlook. There's a download link in this section
- Workspace Email Setup Center

The next menu item says **"Help."** You can use this menu to:

- Find help and tutorials
- Set up Email in MS Outlook
- Email Setup Center
- Visit Go Daddy's support community

Below the drop-down menus, you'll see four rectangular windows that look like *Figure 7*.

Figure 7

1. **All Accounts**: This tab takes you to the same screen as the "Home" button.
2. **View Email**: This screen will give you more detailed information about your email accounts. For example you'll be able to see if you have any forwarders set up, the name of your email plan, and how much disk space your using verses the maximum amount allowed.
3. **View Calendar**: This is a paid feature that you'll never use. It's just a calendar to help you stay organized, but you can do that for free yourself. If you decide to purchase a calendar account, then you can click on this area to manage your calendars.
4. **View Files:** This is another paid feature for online storage. If you have an online storage account, you can manage your files in this area.

Now that you know what all the menus are used for, you're ready to create your first email address. Below those 4 rectangular windows, you'll see a simple menu to help you create/manage email accounts.

- **Create**: Create a single email account.
- **Create Many**: Import a list to create multiple email addresses in bulk.
- **Create Forward**: Create email forwarders.
- **Export**: Export all your email accounts and data into a CSV or Excel file.
- **Delete**: Delete an email address.

Create Your First Email Account

After you're comfortable with the navigation menus, it's time to create your first email account. Click the "**create**" button on the menu bar and a small window will open.

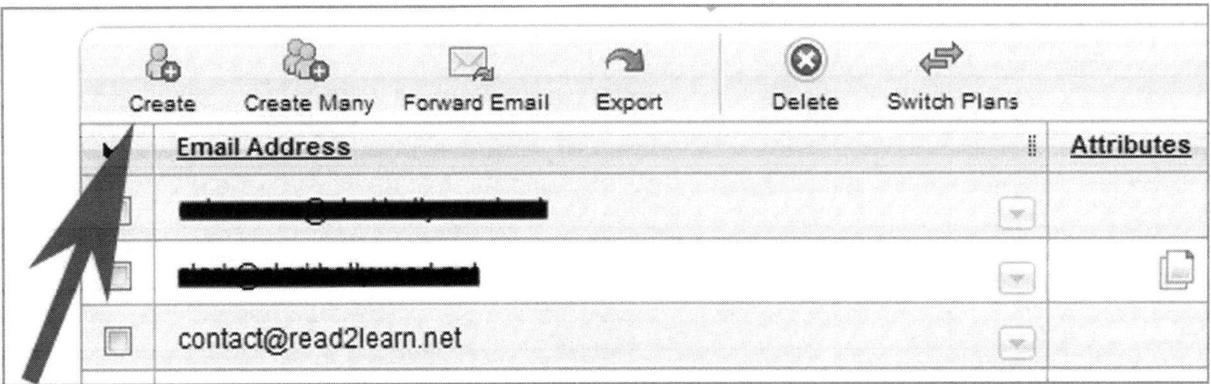

On the next screen you'll need to enter the email address you want, a password, and then confirm the password. Before you click the "create" button to complete the set-up process, make sure that you click the link that says "**Show Additional Options**."

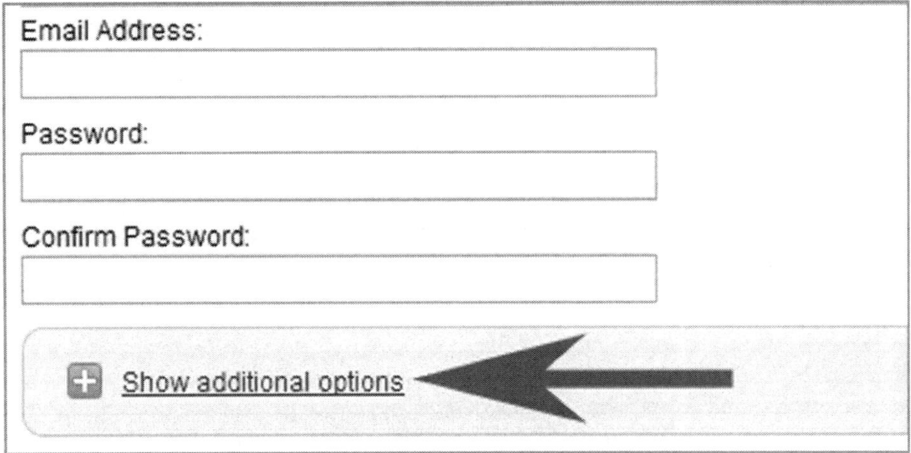

The additional options are important. You'll have the option to:

- Choose which plan to assign to your new email address
- Set a quota for your email inbox (Disk space)
- Make the email address a *catch-all* account (Receives emails sent to misspelled usernames)
- Send copy to (Automatically forward copies to your Gmail account)
- Enable Spam filer
- Enable auto-reply

After you're finished choosing all the additional options you need, click the "create" button. You'll see an alert that says "pending setup" while you're email address is being created. Your email address should be ready to access within 10–20 minutes.

While you're waiting for your email address to complete the setup process, take a look at the right side of your screen. You'll see a box that says "**View By**" and below that you'll see a box that says "**Available Accounts**." (*Figure 8.*)

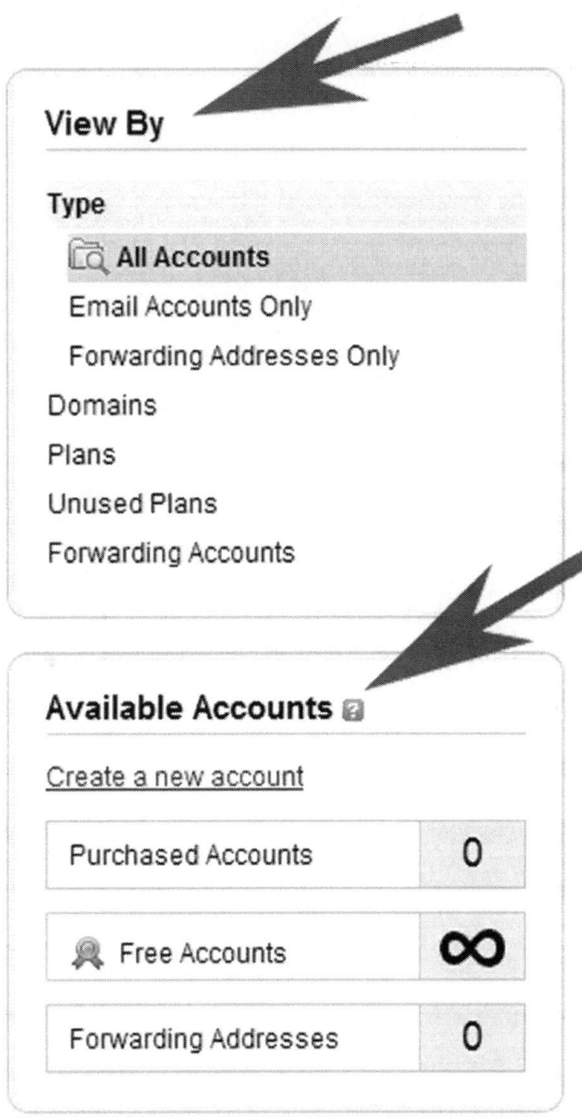

Figure 8

You can use the "View By" box to sort through your emails by domains, plans, unused plans, and forwarding accounts. Feel free to click through that section to see how it works. It's just a sorting feature and there's no way you can break anything by clicking around.

The "Available Accounts" section will show you how many purchased accounts, free accounts, and forwarding addresses you have. There's also a link within this section that you can click to create an email address.

Accessing Your Email

After your email address is set up, you can access your email a few different ways. You'll have the option to launch your email from the *mail management* page you're currently on. Just hover your mouse over your email address and you'll see the option to edit, change your password, and **Launch your email.**

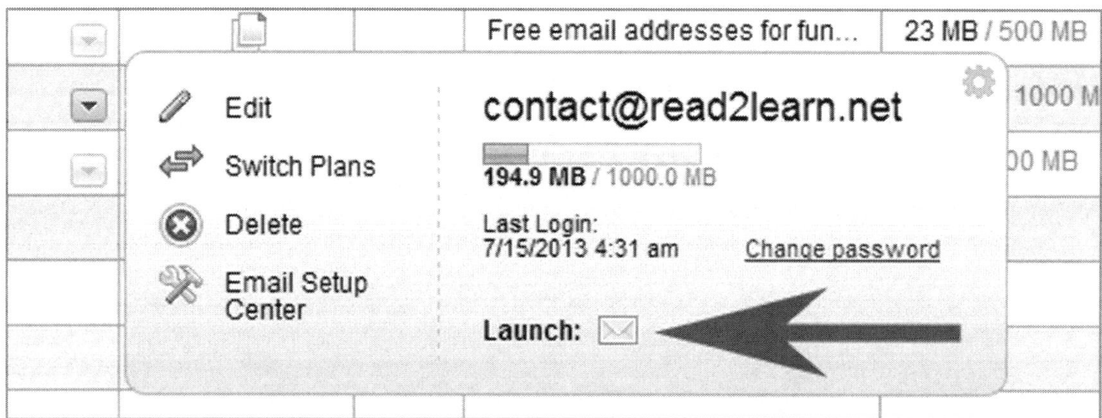

Click the "launch" button, and you'll get forwarded directly into your inbox. When you arrive in your inbox, you'll have additional settings that you can change along with your password and theme.

Login from Your Browser

You can access your email directly from your web browser as well. To access your email, just type "email.YourDomain.com" into your web browser.

(*Example:* **email.read2learn.net**) You'll arrive at a screen that'll prompt you to enter your username and password.

Login from Your Desktop

If you recall earlier, there was an option under the "Tools" section that said "Workspace Tools." There's a download link that'll allow you to access your email directly from your desktop.

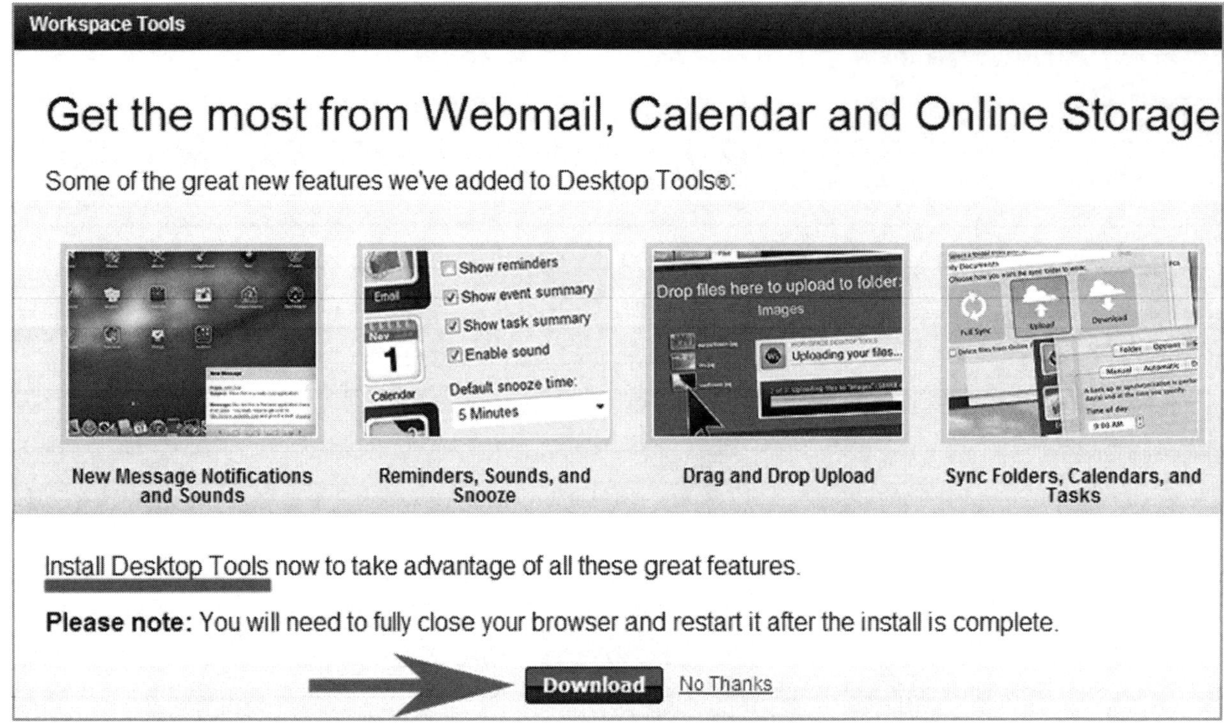

Tips

If you forget your email password, you can log back into your hosting control center and reset the password. You **do not** have to verify your old password to change the password.

You can also use your hosting control center to launch your employee emails and/or send copies of their emails to your inbox. This is good for quality control, and insures that employees are not misusing their company emails.

If you need additional help with your email accounts, visit the help center or just contact customer support over the phone. Phone support is available 24/7/365, so take advantage of it.

In the next chapter we'll discuss File Management and FTP accounts.

Chapter 5

File Management and FTP Accounts

Beneath the email section, you'll see a row for "File Management." This section will provide you with tools that will enable you to transfer files to and from your web hosting account.

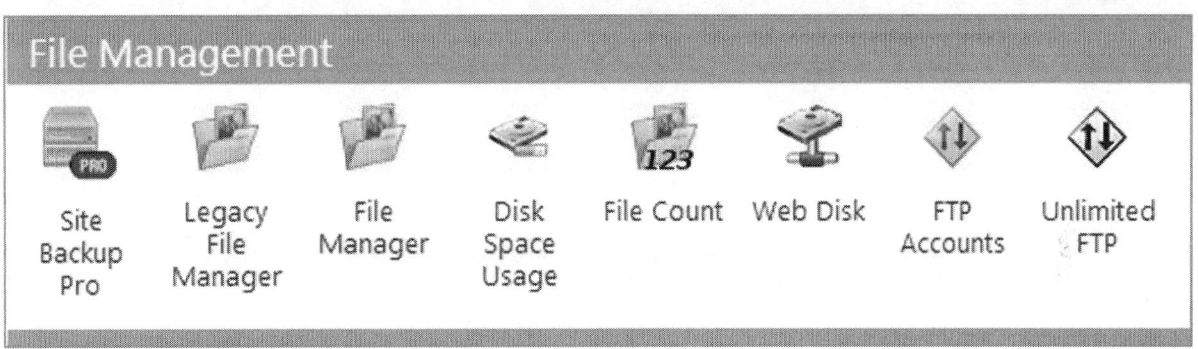

The most common method of transferring files to/from your computer to your web hosting account is via FTP. FTP stands for **File Transfer Protocol**. In simple terms, you'll need an FTP account to download and upload files to your website.

The file management section of cPanel will give you the tools you need to:

- Create FTP accounts
- Delete FTP accounts
- Edit and Manage files using the file manager
- Use a built-in FTP program to transfer small files
- Use a third party FTP program to transfer large files
- Backup and restore your website files

The first icon within the file management section will say "Site Backup Pro." Click that icon and you'll be forwarded to a screen that allows you to download and restore system backups.

Site Backup & Restore

By default, most web hosts will backup your files, databases, and configuration settings automatically every night. Daily, Weekly, and Monthly backups are usually stored on your web hosts servers.

You shouldn't always depend on your web host to backup your files. After you click the "Site Backup Pro" icon, you'll have the option to backup your:

- Full cPanel account
- Website files
- MySQL Database (WordPress settings)
- Email forwarder configurations
- Email filters

If you upgrade to the PRO account, you'll be able to backup:

- Individual files and folders
- Only changed files (recently modified files)

You don't need to upgrade to the PRO account. The free site backup & restore does the same thing and it's free. If you're interested in a PRO account, then click the "more info" link on the right side of the screen for more details and pricing.

The next icon within the file management says Legacy File Manager. Click that icon.

Legacy File Manager

The legacy file manager is a quick way to manage files and directories in your hosting account. You'll have the option to upload files, create new folders, and create new files.

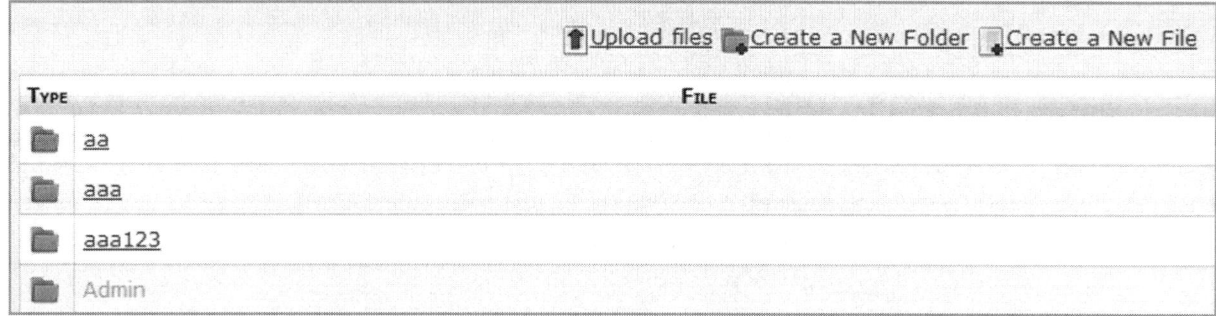

If you click on the folder icon next to the directory, you'll be able to see the contents of that folder. You can upload, download, and work with files on this screen. If you click on the filename next to the folders, you'll see a few options on the right side of the screen. You'll have the option to:

- Delete the folder and all the files under it
- Change permissions

- Rename the folder
- Copy the folder
- Move the folder

After you delete a file, you can click on the trashcan icon to empty the trash. If you accidently delete a file, then you can click the item below the trashcan to restore it.

If you navigate back to the *File Management* area of cPanel, you'll notice the next icon says File Manager. Click that icon and open the file manager.

File Manager

This file manager has more options compared to the *legacy file manager*. You'll see the same options as the legacy file manager such as:

- Add new file
- Add new folder

- Copy & move file
- Upload
- Download
- Delete

This **File Manager** will also allow you to:

- Edit files
- Edit code
- Edit HTML
- Extract and compress files

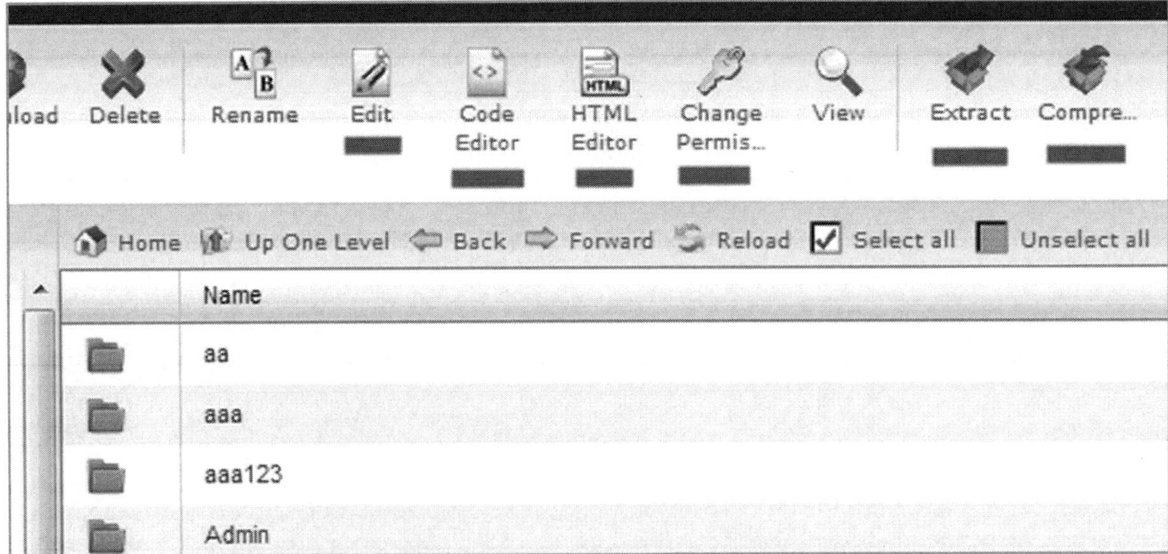

On the left side of the screen, you'll see a list of all your directories. You can navigate to any of these directories to see how many files you have, make edits, or delete files.

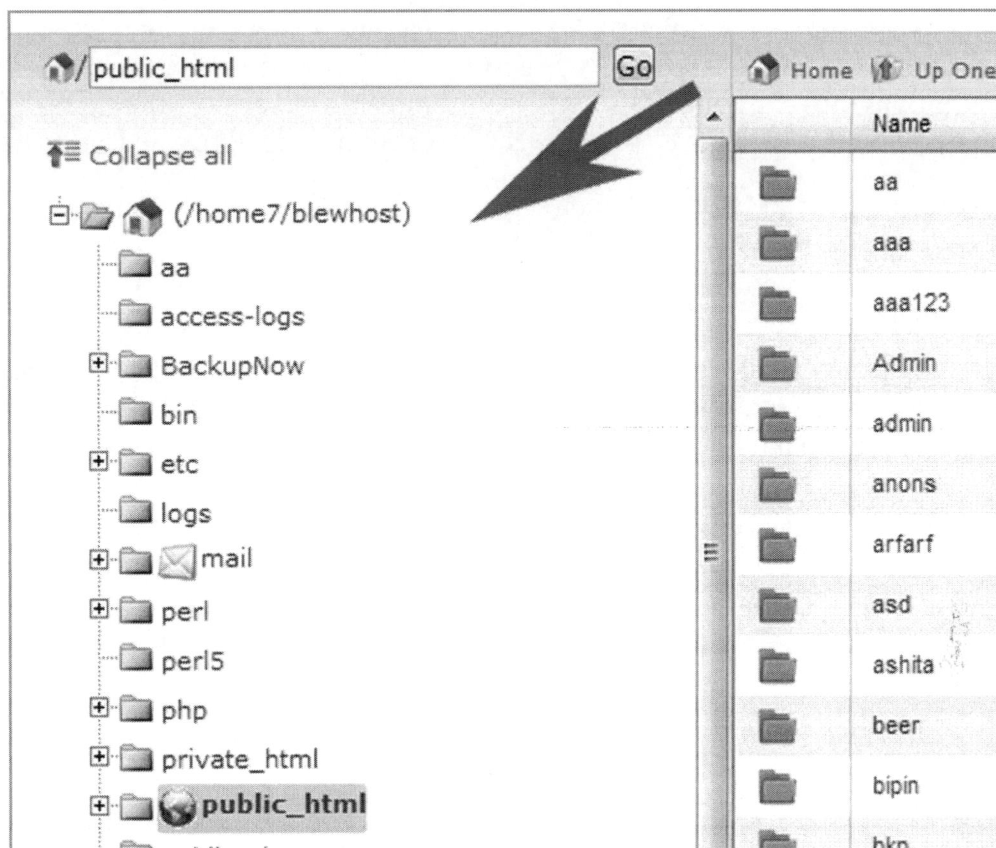

In the middle of the screen you'll see a list of the files for the specified directory. There you'll see the name of the file, size of the file, last time the file was modified, type of file, and the permission settings.

As a WordPress user, you'll probably never need to use the File Manager. You can add WordPress themes, plugins, and upload images directly from your **WordPress dashboard**.

When you install new plugins and themes from your WordPress dashboard, a new folder is automatically created and added to your file manager. When you uninstall and delete a theme or plugin from your WordPress dashboard; the folder is automatically deleted from your file manager.

Some WordPress plugins may require you to edit a file. For example, there's a plugin called "*Hyper Cache Extended*" that requires you to add a line a code to a specific file for the plugin to work. I actually use that plugin, and that's the only time I've ever had to use my file manger to change anything.

Your *WordPress Dashboard* and *File Manager* are **synced** together. So whatever new files you add, delete, or upload using your WordPress dashboard will be reflected in your file manager. Most WordPress users use the file manager to edit files rather than uploading new ones.

If you do decide to manually upload files to your server, make sure that the files are in connection with your hosted website. You're **not** supposed to use a shared hosting account to upload random files for online storage. Read the terms of service or contact your web host if you're not sure what type of files you can and cannot upload to a shared server.

Navigate back to your cPanel homepage. You'll notice that the next icon on the file management section says "Disk Space Usage."

Disk Space Usage

The cPanel *Disk Usage Viewer* provides an overview of the disk space that your account is using. It shows disk usage totals for your account's directories and all of its databases rather than for individual files or databases.

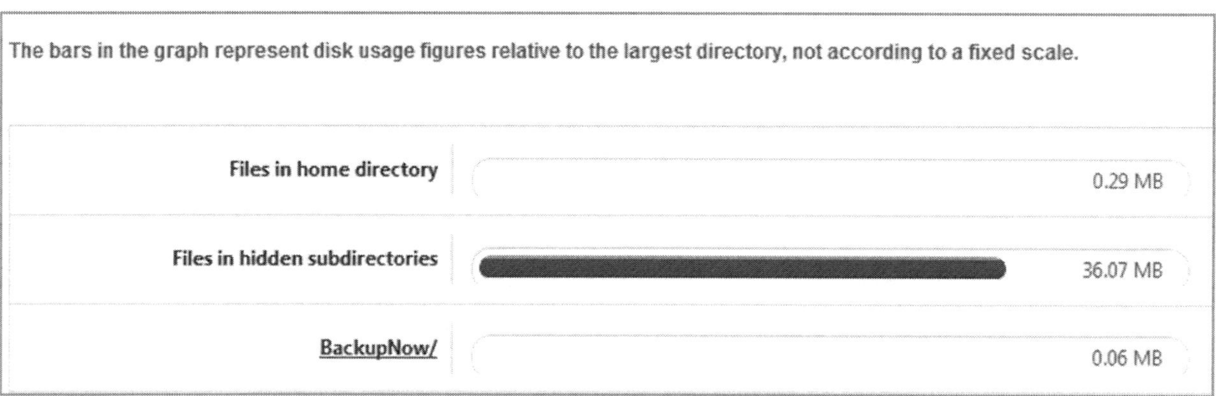

Use the *File Manager* to see disk usage data for individual files, and the *MySQL* and *PostgreSQL* main pages to see data for individual databases. If your hosting account offers unlimited disk space, then you don't really have to worry about how much space you're using.

If your hosting provider offers limited disk space, then you can use the "disk space usage" option to see how much disk space you're using. You'll notice that most WordPress websites don't require that much disk space at all.

The next icon on the file management row says "File Count." Click that icon and you'll get forwarded to a new window.

File Count

On this page you'll see a total number of how many files you have on your hosting account. The count is generated once every week, so your file count may not be accurate. You can contact technical support if you need an accurate file count.

Total Count for blewhost.com: 7896

Count	Directory
2276	/home7/blewhost/tmp/pear/cache
1643	/home7/blewhost/.cpanel/datastore
793	/home7/blewhost/.cpanel
186	/home7/blewhost/.cpcpan/pingtimes

This page will show you a list of all your directories and how many files are in each directory. The list will be sorted by the directory with the most files to the least.

The next icon on the file management row says “Web Disk.” Click that icon to create a web disk account.

Web Disk

The *Web Disk* feature allows you to easily drag and drop files to your hosting account. Once your *Web Disk* is configured, you can then drag and drop files directly from your computer making it easier to update and manage your site.

Create Web Disk Account

Login: @ blewhost.com

New Password:

Password (Again):

Strength (why?): Very Weak (0/100) Password Generator

Directory: /

Create

To create a web disk account, simply choose a login, password, and click the create button. If you're going to drag and drop files, make sure that they're in connection with your hosted website. Web hosting providers will not allow inappropriate use of their network for online storage.

The next icon on the list says "FTP Accounts." Before you click that icon, I want to explain more about FTP accounts and what they are used for.

FTP Accounts

All web hosting accounts come with at least one FTP account. You'll notice that you're prompted to choose a FTP username and password when you set up your web hosting account. You can use your FTP username and password with stand-alone **FTP clients** to download and upload files to your web hosting account.

An example of a stand-alone FTP client is **Filezilla**. Filezilla is free to use, and it's compatible with Microsoft windows. If you're using a MAC, then you can use a FTP client like **CuteFTP** or **Rbrowser**.

After you choose a FTP client you'll be able to connect to your website via FTP. To connect via FTP, you'll need the following information ready:

Host: Enter your websites domain name into this section or ftp.yourdomain.com

FTP Username: This will be the same as your cPanel username. **

FTP Password: This will be same as your cPanel password.

Port: You should be able to connect via FTP without entering any port information. If you can't connect, trying using port 21.

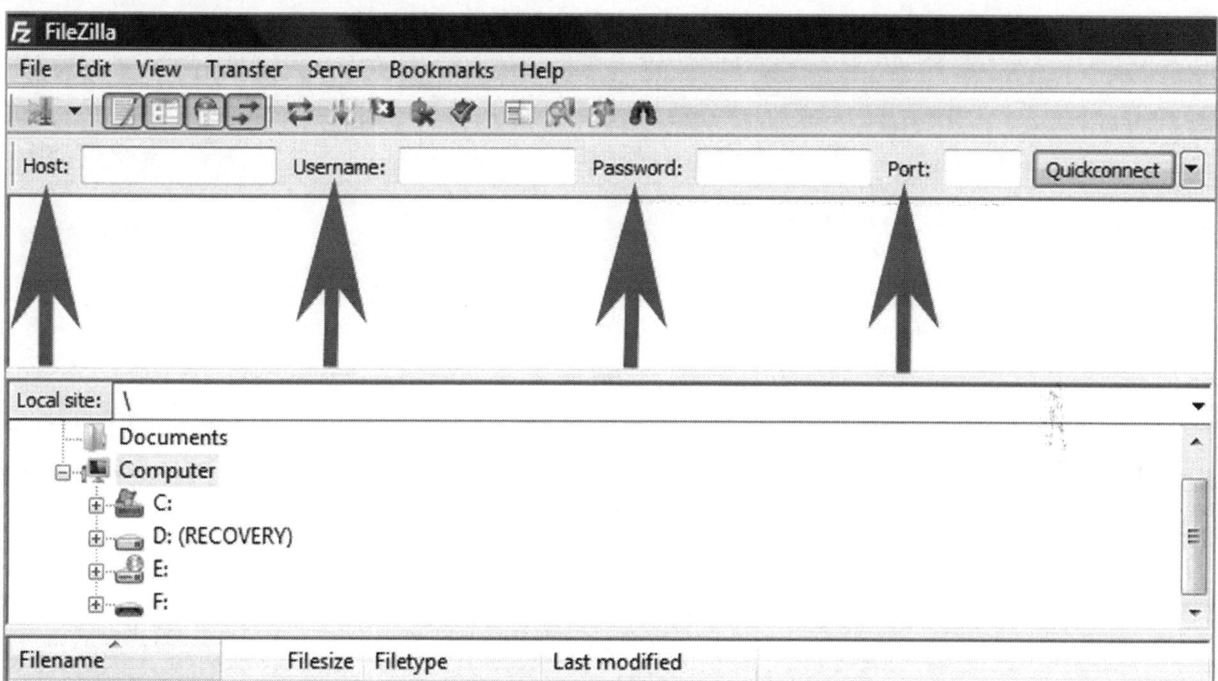

After you're done entering all the necessary information, click the connect/quick connect button. After you're connected via FTP, the left window will show all the files on your computer. The window on the right will show all the files on your web server. You can use your FTP client to transfer files between your computer and web server.

FTP clients are ideal if you need to work with very large files. If you just need to upload images, WordPress themes, or WordPress plugins; then you can do that from your WordPress dashboard. WordPress already has a built-in user-friendly FTP program.

If you're familiar with WordPress, then you know that you can upload almost anything from your desktop by using the "media" tab within WordPress. **The process of transferring files from your desktop to your website is called FTP.**

If you're having trouble logging in via FTP; check to make sure you've entered in your information correctly. If you're still having trouble connecting to your website via FTP, then contact your web host for assistance.

***Go Daddy will prompt you to set up an FTP username and password when you initially set up your WordPress website. Your FTP username and password will be different from your Go Daddy login information.*

As mentioned earlier, you'll have at least one FTP account already set up by default. You probably won't need more than one FTP account if you're the only person that makes changes to your website.

When should you create another FTP account? Well if you have a person helping you with your website and they want to connect via FTP, you should create a separate FTP login for them.

Keep in mind that your **main FTP** login has the same username and password as your cPanel account. If you give someone your main FTP login, you're giving them the login to your cPanel account too which is a security risk.

How to Create a New FTP Account

Click the icon within the file management section that says *FTP Accounts*. On the next screen, you'll be able to add a new FTP account by:

- Choosing a FTP login name.
- Choosing a password for the new FTP account.
- Choose a specific directory you want the new user to have access to. You can also leave this section blank, and the user will access to any files and directories in the *public_html*.
- Specify a quota limit or set this to unlimited. The quota limit will restrict the designated FTP account from uploading more than the specified amount in MB.
- Click "Create FTP Account" and you're done.

Add FTP Account

Login: @blewhost.com

Password:

Password (Again):

Strength (?): Very Weak (0/100) Password Generator

Directory: /home7/blewhost/

Quota: 2000 MB

Unlimited

Create FTP Account

After the FTP account is created, you'll see the new FTP account listed on the same screen down below. You'll see the login information, the path/directory for that FTP account, the quota for the account, and actions.

It's important to note that you **cannot** edit FTP accounts; you can only delete them. So if you want to change the login information for a FTP account you created, just delete it instead and create a new one.

Actually if you're only creating a new FTP account because someone is helping you transfer files, you should delete that FTP account once they're done. If they need to access your website via FTP in the future, then create a new FTP account for them.

Navigate back to your cPanel home page and click the last item within the *file management* section that says "Unlimited FTP."

Unlimited FTP

The Unlimited FTP tool is a built-in FTP client**. You can use this tool to FTP files from your desktop to your web host the same as Filezilla. This is an ideal solution if you need to upload or download small files. If you need to work with a lot of large files, then you should use a stand-alone FTP client like Filezilla.

***You'll probably get a security warning when using this tool because you're opening a gateway between your computer and the web server.*

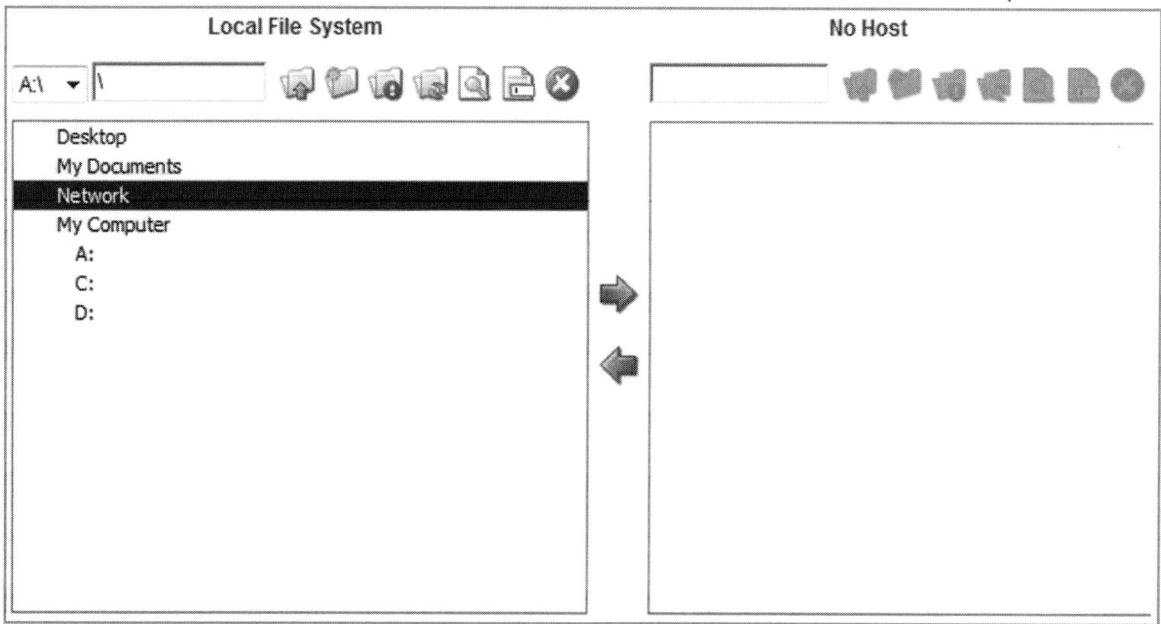

You'll probably notice that this tool has the same layout as Filezilla. On the left side of the screen you'll see a list of the local files on your computer. On the right side of the screen you'll see a list of files on your web host. You can transfer files from your desktop computer to your web host using this tool.

You'll need software called "Java" installed on your computer for this tool to work. If you don't have Java installed, your computer will prompt you to install it. There's also a download link on the page that you can click if you need to install Java on your computer.

Go Daddy Users

Go Daddy has similar tools for file management, but they're just located in different sections. If you look at *Figure 9*, you'll see an icon for File Manager, Java FTP Client (*Unlimited FTP*), FTP Users, and Disk Space Usage.

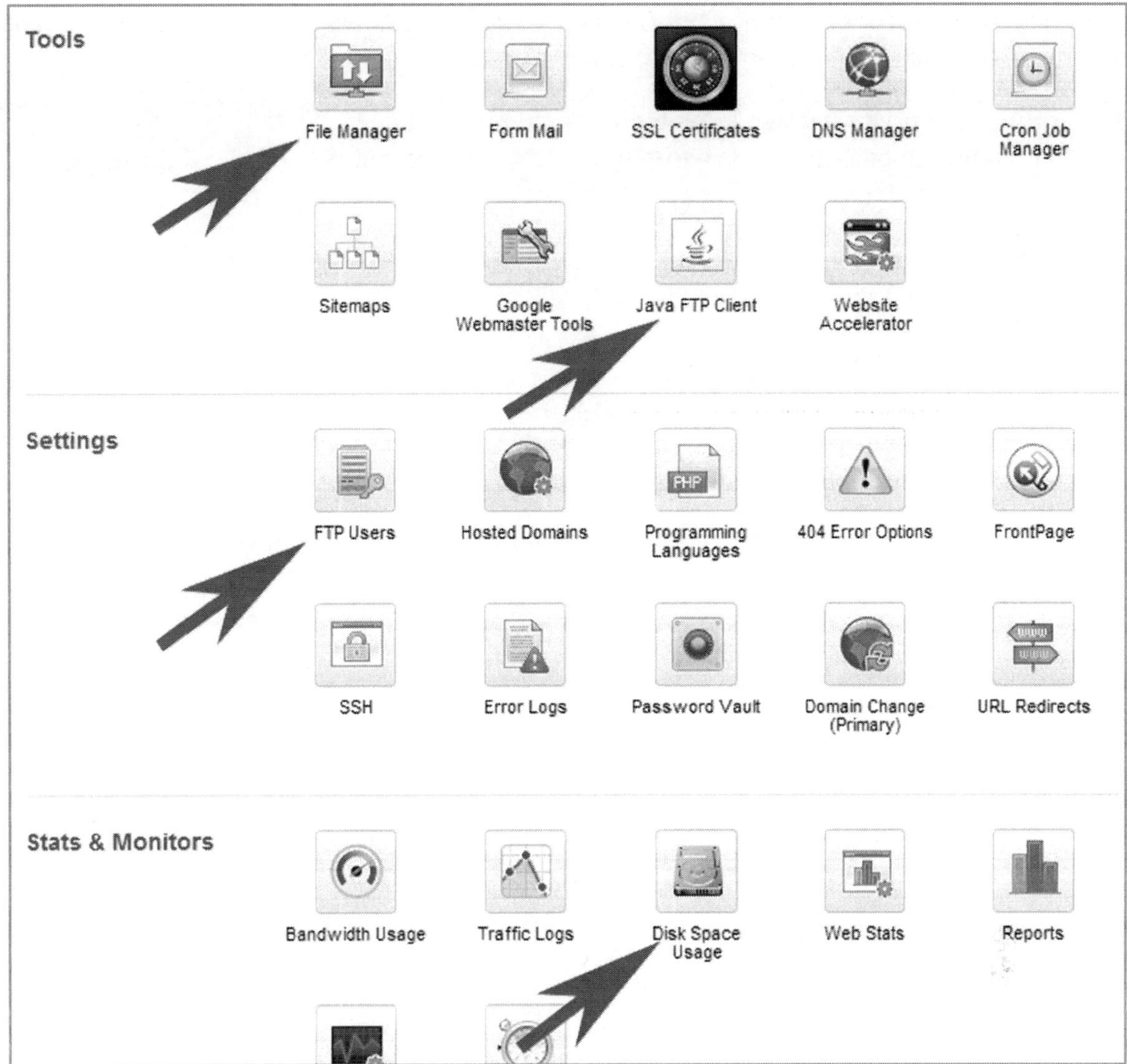

Figure 9

The most important feature is the **FTP users** feature. If you click that icon, you'll be able to create and/or delete FTP accounts the same way you can with cPanel.

Go Daddy also has a built-in FTP feature called **Java FTP Client**. As mentioned earlier, these built-in FTP features are just a miniature version of a stand-alone FTP client like Filezilla. You probably won't ever use this feature to transfer files to and from your website.

You can transfer and delete 90% of files directly from your WordPress dashboard which is the easy way. Some people like to upload WordPress plugins, themes, and images via Filezilla but that's using WordPress on "hard mode."

The only notable feature missing from Go Daddy's Hosting Control Center is the *Site Backup Pro* feature. Go Daddy will automatically backup your website for you.

If you want to manually backup your website, then you can use Filezilla (or another stand-alone FTP client) to transfer your website files to your computer or a USB flash drive. You can also use a WordPress plugin called "*WordPress BackUp to Dropbox*."

That covers everything within the file management section of your cPanel. In this chapter you learned how to:

- Backup and restore files
- Create and manage FTP accounts
- Log into stand-alone FTP clients like Filezilla
- Use cPanel's File Manager to upload, download and manage files
- Check your disk space usage
- Get a "file count"
- Set up a web disk accounts

In the next chapter you'll learn how to check your websites statistics.

Chapter 6

Statistics

cPanel offers several tools to check your website stats. The "statistics" section of cPanel offers tools that will enable you to check who's visiting your website, bandwidth usage, and an *error log* option that'll show you problems with your website.

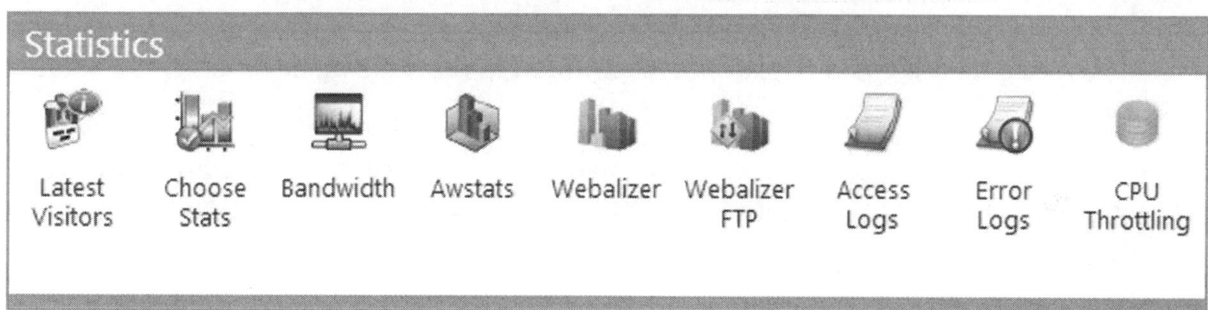

You'll be surprised at how many people don't realize their hosting provider has static tools available. Some people get frustrated trying to use the Google Analytics stats tool, but all the tools you need are already available on cPanel.

In this chapter I'll show you how to work with some of these tools. I'll also give you a few links with more information if you need help troubleshooting these tools.

The first icon you'll see on your stats section says "Latest Visitors." Click that icon and you'll get forwarded to a very basic stats page.

Latest Visitors

Once you arrive to the *Latest Visitors Stats* page, you'll have to select a domain name that you want to see the stats for.

This tool will show you the last **1000 hits** on your website. If one person visits your website and clicks around 50 times; this will count as 50 hits/1000 hits.

This simple tool will show you:

- The IP Address of the visitor
- The URL they visited on your website
- The time they visited

- The website that referred them to your website
- The user agent/program that accessed your website (Mozilla, Google Bot, etc.)

If you want more comprehensive statistics, go back to your cPanel dashboard and click the icon that says "Choose Stats."

Choose Stats

After you click the "Choose Stats" icon, you'll get forwarded to a screen that says "Choose Log Programs." This function allows you to choose which stats program to use when viewing your websites statistics.

All the statistic reports are updated every 24 hours, and the bandwidth information is updated every 6 hours. You must have stats **enabled** in the stats manager at least 24 hours before any stats will be compiled.

On this page you'll have the option to enable a stats program called **Awstats** and **Webalizer**. You'll also see a list of your domain names, and you can choose which domain name to activate the stats program for.

Enabled	Domain
☑ awstats ☑ webalizer	**blewhost.com**
	SAVE CHANGES

After you enable the stats software, click "Save Changes" and navigate back to your cPanel dashboard. The next icon on that stats row says "Bandwidth." Click the bandwidth icon to see your bandwidth usage.

Bandwidth

After you click the bandwidth icon, you'll get forwarded to a page that has 4 different graphs. There'll be a graph showing you your bandwidth usage for:

- Last 24 hours
- Past 7 days
- Past 30 days
- Past Year

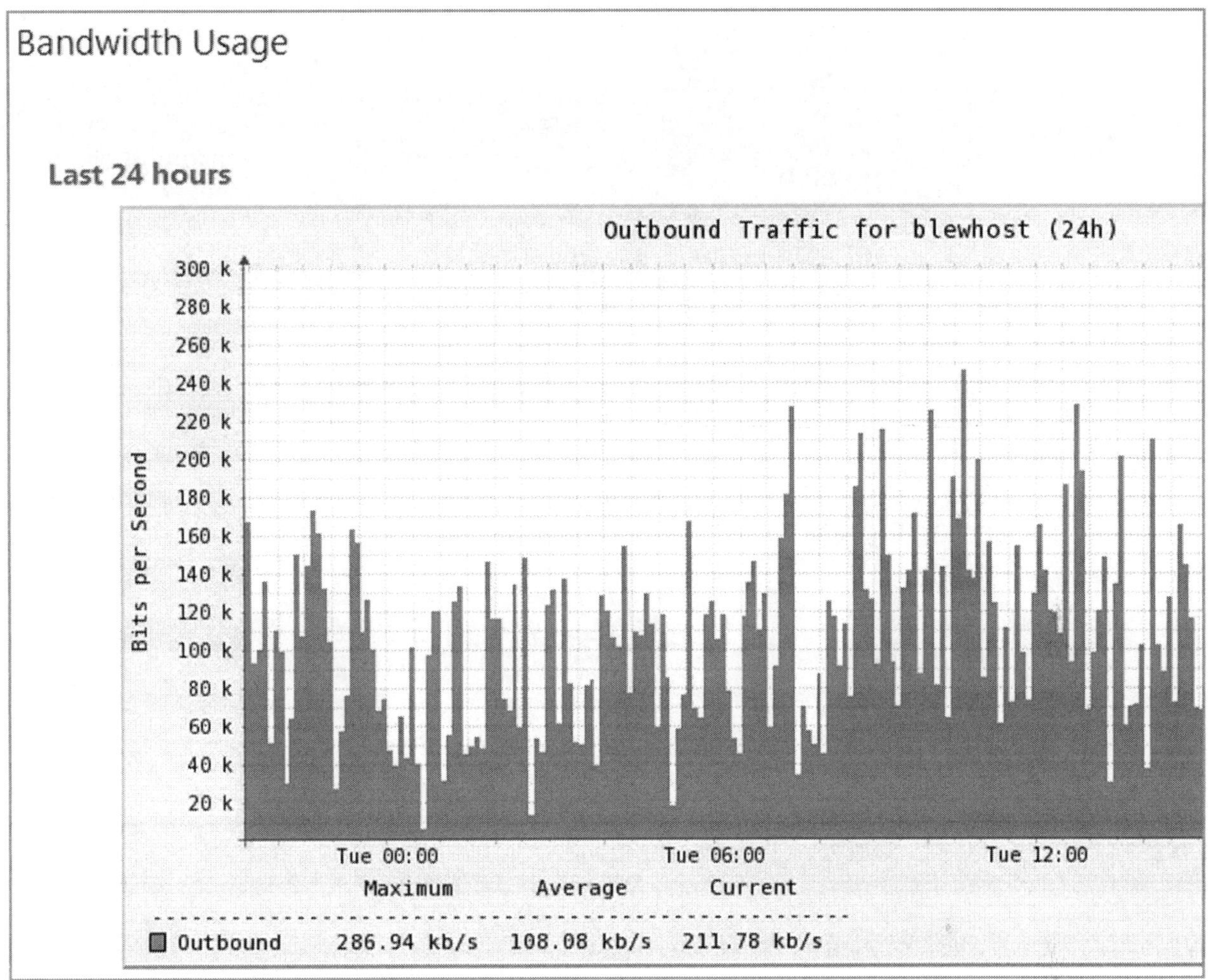

If your hosting account has **unlimited** bandwidth/GB file transfer, then you don't have to worry about your bandwidth usage. If you plan on moving your website over to a *virtual private server* or a *dedicated server* with limited bandwidth; then you should keep an eye on your bandwidth to make sure you don't go over your allowed limit.

Go back to the statistics section and the next icon on the list says Awstats. If you recall earlier, you were asked to choose a stats program for your domain name. If you chose Awstats, then you can check your stats by clicking the Awstats icon.

Awstats

Awstats uses a lot of graphics and provides you with more information about visitors compared to the "Latest Visitors" option we used earlier. The top left of the screen will display which domain name you're checking statistics for. Below that you'll see links that you can click to navigate through your stats faster.

On the top of the main screen you'll see the last time your statistics were updated. You can also use the drop down menu to choose previous monthly reports. If you'd like your reports generated in another language, you can click the picture of the "flag icons" on the top right. The current languages available are:

- French
- German
- Italian
- Dutch
- Spanish
- English

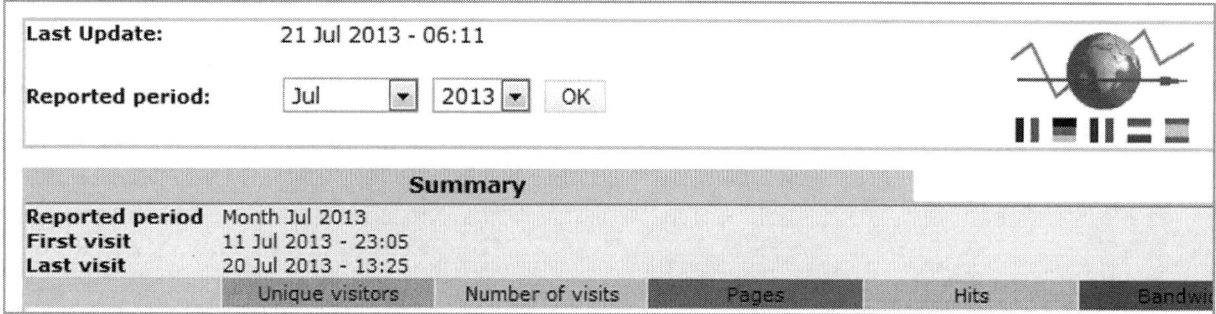

Here's some important statistical information this tool provides:

- Unique visitors

- Number of visits
- Number of pages visited
- How many total hits
- Bandwidth usage
- Top 25 countries that visit your website
- Average time visitors stay on your website
- Top 25 pages on your website visited
- Website that referred visitors to your website
- Keyword phrases that people are using to find your website

It's a good idea to print out your reports and check your progress over time. You can use this information to figure out which parts of your website are the most interesting to your visitors.

If you want to learn more information about Awstats, you can visit their website and download their PDF documentation here: http://awstats.sourceforge.net

The next icon on the stats section says "Webalizer." You have the option to use this stats tool as well; so click the icon to see if you like this tool better.

Webalizer

After you click the Webalizer icon, you'll get forwarded to a page with a brief summary of your stats for the month. Some of the information included on this summary page includes:

- Daily average page views
- Daily average website hits
- Monthly totals

Summary by Month										
Month	Daily Avg				Monthly Totals					
	Hits	Files	Pages	Visits	Sites	KBytes	Visits	Pages	Files	Hits
Jul 2013	0	0	0	0	3	3	2	3	3	5
Jun 2013	0	0	0	0	4	3	6	6	10	10
May 2013	0	0	0	0	3	5	3	3	4	4
Apr 2013	0	0	0	0	0	0	0	0	0	0
Mar 2013	0	0	0	0	0	0	0	0	0	0
Feb 2013	0	0	0	0	0	0	0	0	0	0

If you'd like to see more detailed information, you'll have to click on the name of the month you're interested in viewing. You'll get forwarded to another page with more in depth information about that particular month.

If you need help understanding Webalizer's main headings and definitions; then you can visit their website for more information: http://www.webalizer.org/webalizer_help.html

The next item on the statistics row says "Webalizer FTP." This tool does that same thing as the main Webalizer icon, but it uses the FTP protocol. You probably won't ever use "Webalizer FTP" because it's just a complicated way of using the same tool.

The next icon on that statistics row says "Access Logs." Click that icon to access your raw access logs.

Access Log

The access log is a raw log that's in text form. The file will be large and hard to read which is why it's towards the end of the stats row. The other programs like Awstats and Webalizer interprets this data for you, so you're better off using those programs.

You can use the "Raw Access Logs" menu to download a zipped version of the server's access logs for your site. Since the file will be compressed, you'll need a program that will be able to uncompress the files. Once you unzip the file, the raw access logs will allow you to see who has visited your website **without** displaying graphs, charts or other graphics.

If you want a simple way to track your website statistics, then I recommend using **Awstats** or the **Jetpack Stats** feature that's already included within your WordPress dashboard. The *Access Log* feature will be too confusing and time consuming.

The next icon on your stats row says "Error Logs." Click that icon.

Error Logs

This feature will show you problems that people have had when trying to access your website. The error log is a **shared log** meaning that errors from all websites hosted on the same server will be displayed as well as those for your website.

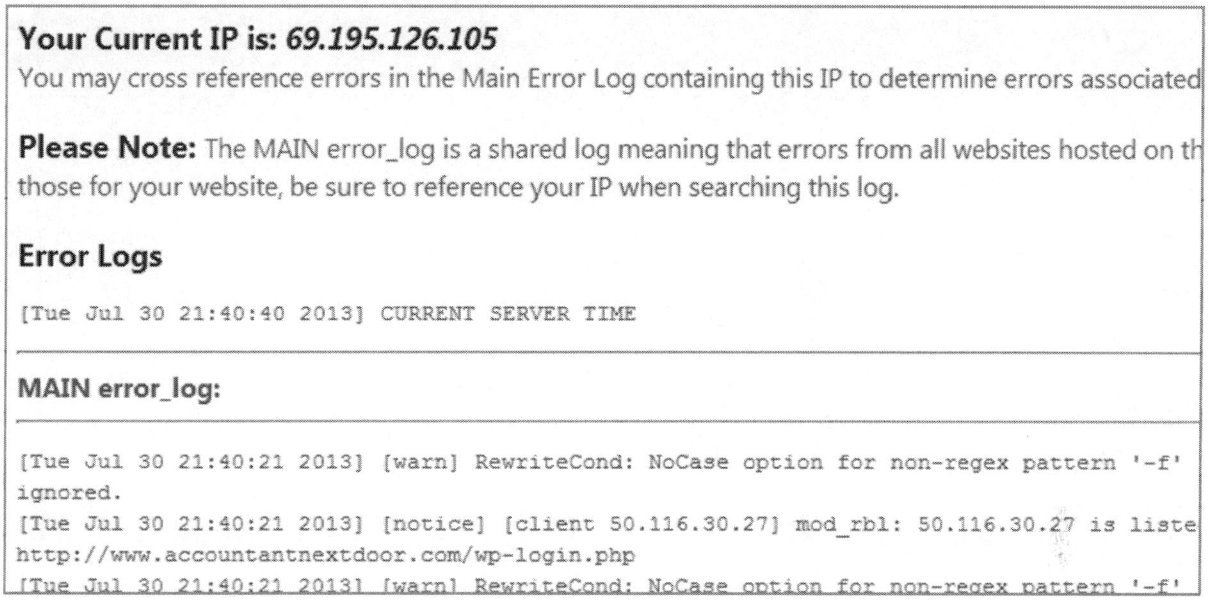

Your Current IP is: *69.195.126.105*

You may cross reference errors in the Main Error Log containing this IP to determine errors associated

Please Note: The MAIN error_log is a shared log meaning that errors from all websites hosted on th those for your website, be sure to reference your IP when searching this log.

Error Logs

```
[Tue Jul 30 21:40:40 2013] CURRENT SERVER TIME
```

MAIN error_log:

```
[Tue Jul 30 21:40:21 2013] [warn] RewriteCond: NoCase option for non-regex pattern '-f'
ignored.
[Tue Jul 30 21:40:21 2013] [notice] [client 50.116.30.27] mod_rbl: 50.116.30.27 is liste
http://www.accountantnextdoor.com/wp-login.php
[Tue Jul 30 21:40:21 2013] [warn] RewriteCond: NoCase option for non-regex pattern '-f'
```

At the top of the screen you'll see your current IP address. You need to reference your IP address when searching the error log to make sure the errors are from your website and not someone else sharing the server.

You can use this tool if your clients are having problems accessing certain parts of your website. This can help you troubleshoot some issues on your own before contacting your web host for support.

This tool will be able to tell you if a download link is broken or if images are missing. For example, you might have a page up with a broken download link to a book. If you've forgotten that you changed a download link to a new location, this tool will tell you that the file is broken and doesn't exist. This information will allow you to fix the error.

The last item on the statistics row says "CPU throttling." What's CPU throttling?

CPU Throttling

CPU Throttling means that your web host has automatically tied your account to its own dedicated core temporarily to keep your account from using too many resources. In simple terms, your website is sucking up way too many resources and you're slowing down the other websites that are sharing the same server.

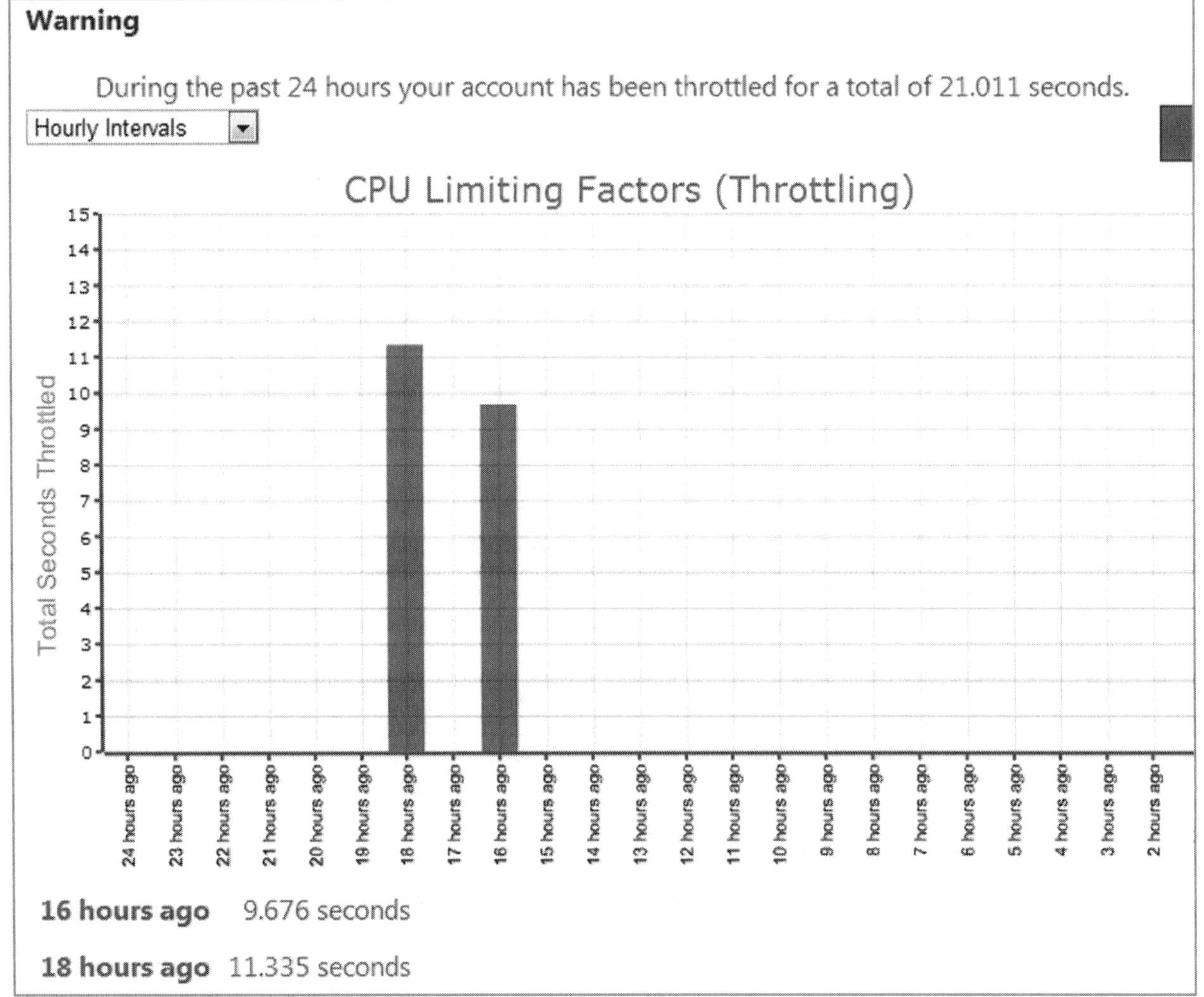

Throttling is caused by:

- Badly coded WordPress themes, add-ons, or plugins that aren't loading properly. (If you just added a new component to your Website, you may want to remove it to see if that new component caused your site to suddenly perform slowly.)
- Queries that return inordinately large dataset results. (eg: 100,000 records)
- Any process that uses too much RAM.
- Too many simultaneous connections like Downloads, FTP, IMAP, or PHP, Videos, etc.

Click the "CPU Throttling" icon to see if any limiting factors have been placed on your account. If your website is well organized and you're not experimenting with homemade themes and plugins, you shouldn't run into this problem. If you continue to suck up too many resources on a shared hosting account, then your hosting account could get suspended until you fix the problem.

Check Your Statistics with Go Daddy

Go Daddy has similar statistic features, but I think it's more simplified. Log into your Go Daddy hosting account and click the "Launch" button on the web hosting row. You'll see an icon for:

- Error Logs
- Bandwidth Usage
- Traffic Logs
- Web Stats
- Reports
- System Processes
- Website Performance

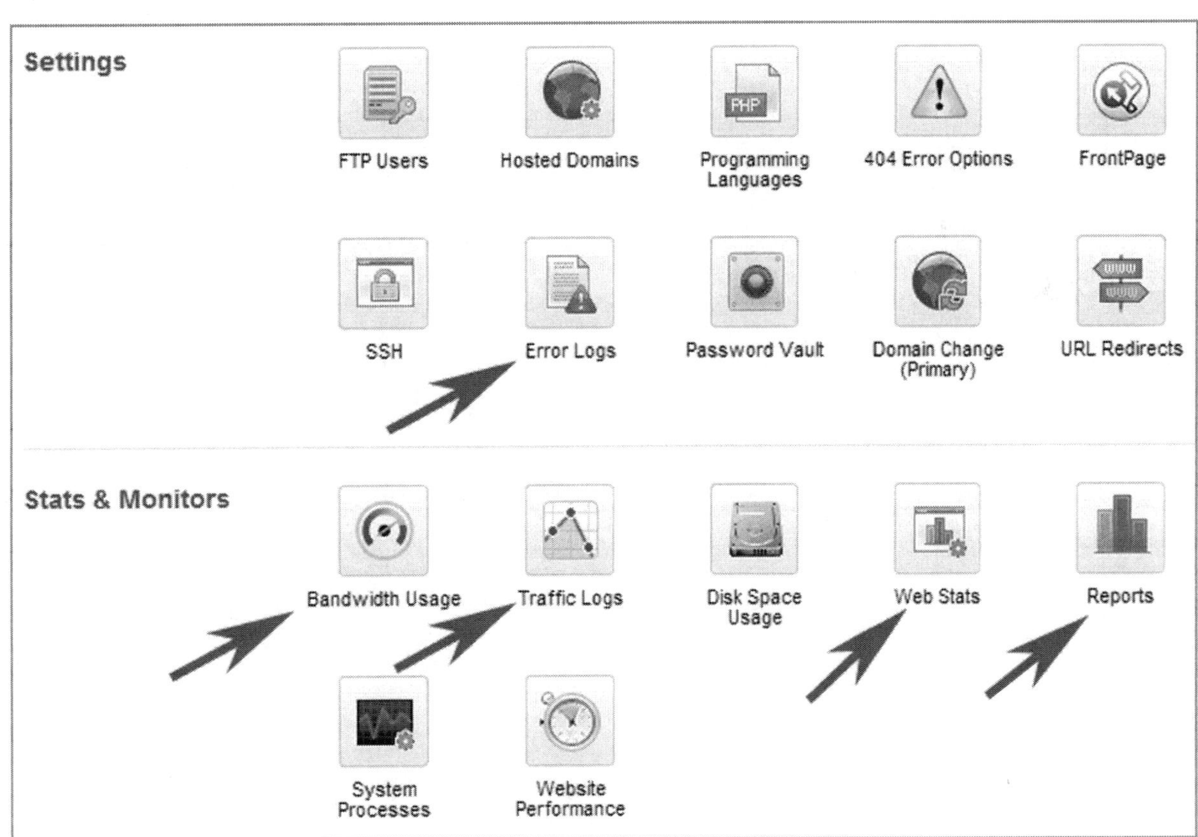

Error Logs Icon

Click the *Error Logs* icon. To start error log data collection, you have to click the *Update* button. To view error logs, click the *Error Logs* link.

When you enable error logs on your hosting plan, Go Daddy will start collecting error log data for a seven-day period. After seven days, collection stops and your error logs are deleted. If you start a new collection during an existing one, your error logs are deleted and collection starts again.

Bandwidth Usage Icon

Click the bandwidth icon and you'll get forwarded to a page with a graph. The "Bandwidth Usage Statistics" graph displays your hosting account's bandwidth consumption. Daily bandwidth usage is shown in megabytes (MB).

The date range of the bandwidth usage is shown at the top of the chart. You can change the chart type from Bar, Line or Area. Click the different options to determine which graph is easier for you to read.

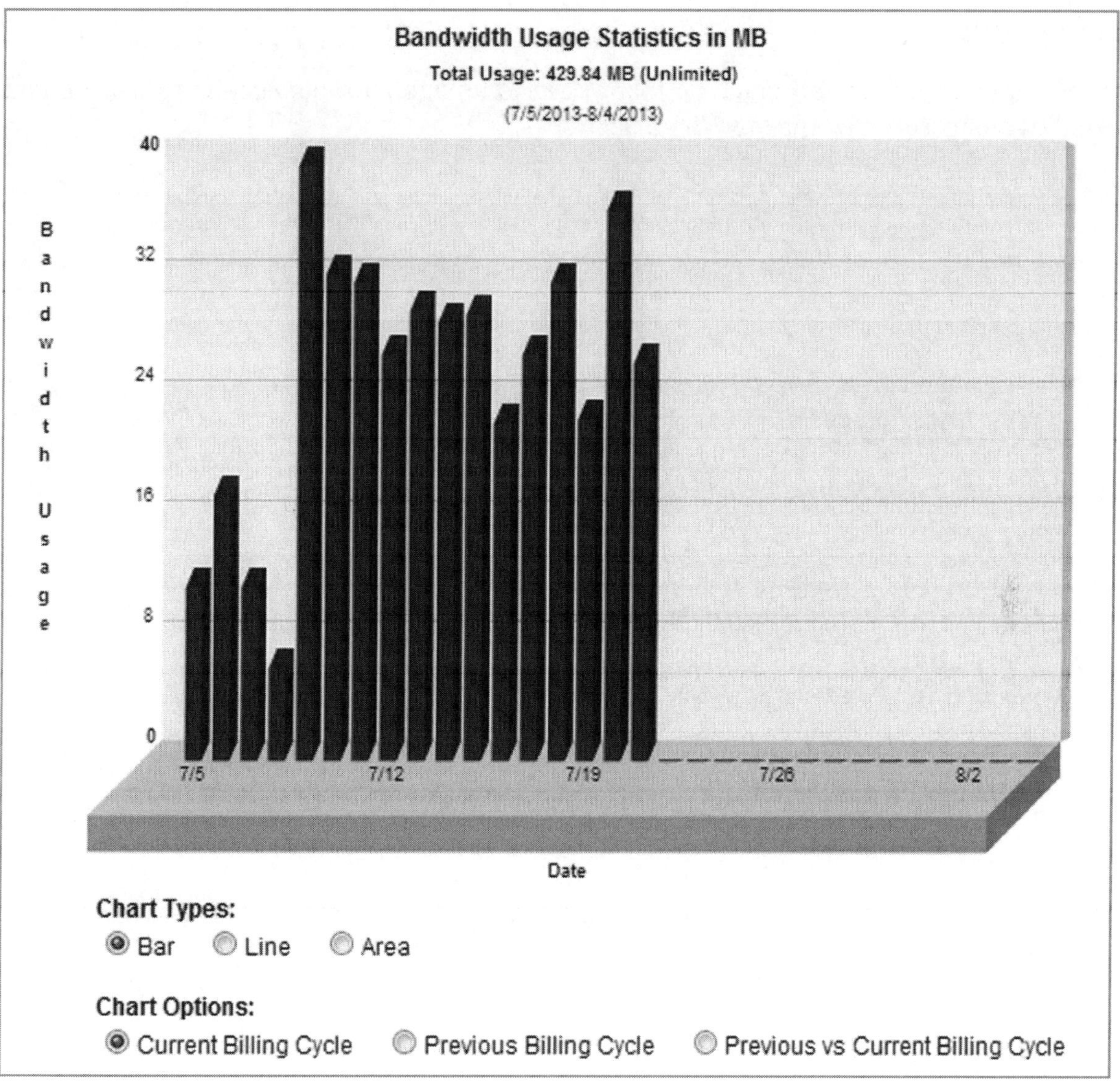

You'll also have a few more chart options such as:

- Current Billing Cycle: Displays the current billing cycle's usage.
- Previous Billing Cycle: Displays the previous billing cycle's usage.
- Previous vs. Current Billing Cycle: Compares usage between previous and current billing cycle.

Go Daddy's shared hosting plans come with unlimited bandwidth, so you don't have to worry about running out of bandwidth. If you're just curious to find out how much bandwidth you're using, then you can use this tool.

Traffic Logs Icon

Click the traffic logs icon and you'll be forwarded to a page with instructions showing you how to download the Raw Apache Web Logs.

If you recall earlier, "Raw web logs" are written in a text file without graphics and are difficult to read. If you really want to see this text file, you'll have to access your file manager and click "Apache Logs." There you'll see the logs from the past 30 days.

Web Stats Icon

Click the web stats icon and you'll get forwarded to a page that'll allow you to **enable** your web statistics. After you click the enable button, you'll get an alert that says, "*Web Statistics Account Update Submitted! These changes usually take 7 minutes. However, it may take up to 10 minutes for these changes to take effect. These time frames are estimates and not guaranteed.*"

After you web statistics are fully activated, you'll be able to start viewing your web stats for the specified website. You'll need to allow your web host up to **24 hours** to start collecting data for your website traffic. If you click the web stats icon again, you'll have the option to disable your web stats and change your login password to your web stats section.

By default, the login to your web stats section is your FTP username and password. To login in and view your web stats, click the icon that says "Reports."

Reports Icon

Since you've just recently activated your Web stats, you won't see any web stats yet. You'll see a screen that says "*You have recently enabled statistics for your hosting account, but statistics have not yet begun to be collected for your site. This process may take up to twenty four hours.*"

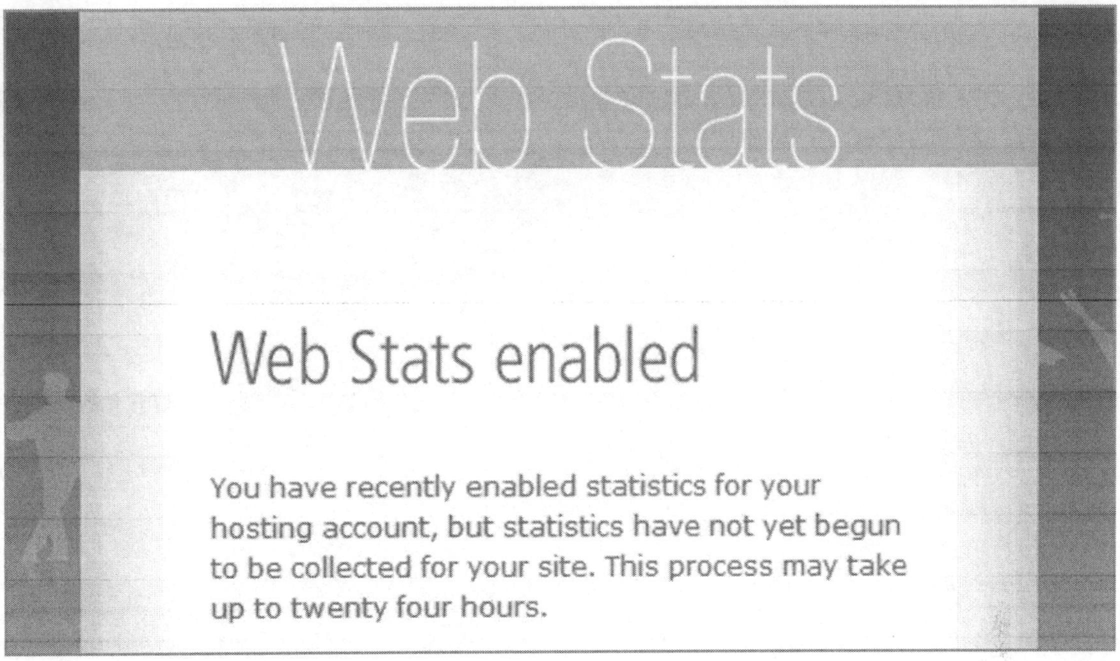

Web Stats

Web Stats enabled

You have recently enabled statistics for your hosting account, but statistics have not yet begun to be collected for your site. This process may take up to twenty four hours.

After 24 hours, you'll see some basic easy to understand graphs explaining your websites traffic. You can use this tool along with the *Jetpack WordPress Stats* feature to check on your websites stats.

System Processes Icon

This tool shows you if someone is currently accessing your site via the web or FTP. If you have other FTP users, then you'll be able to see when they logged into your website and what they're up too.

You can also use this tool to "End all" sessions and kick everybody off your website. If you're the only person who makes changes to your website, then you should only see your activity within this section.

Website Accelerator Icon

Click this icon and you'll have the option to activate a free website accelerator. After you click the activate button, you'll receive a *congratulations* notification saying that they're shifting your website into high gear. You'll need to wait at least an hour for the changes to take effect.

After you log back in, Go Daddy will tell you how much faster your website is. There's also an *advanced metrics* option that'll show you a comparison between your old website performance and your accelerated performance. (**You need Go Daddy's* ***Ultimate Hosting Plan*** *to activate this feature.*)

That covers everything within your statistics section. In the next chapter we'll discuss the security features available through cPanel.

Chapter 7

Security

The security section of cPanel is mostly composed of advanced features that you probably won't use. It's still good to know what these features are so you'll have a well rounded understanding of cPanel.

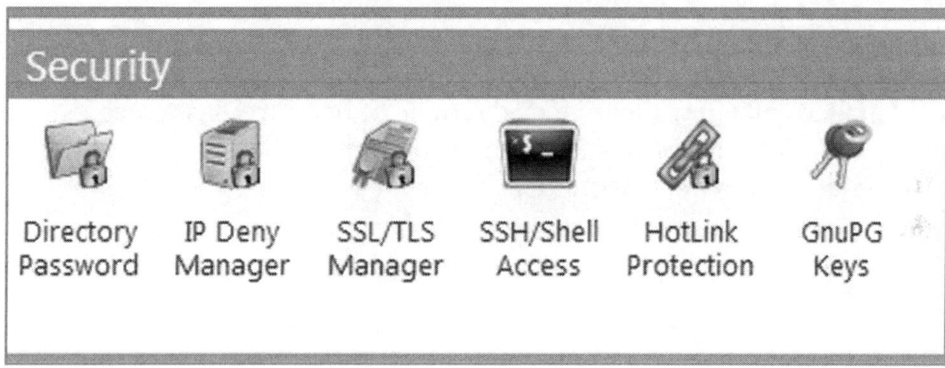

<u>Directory Password</u>

The first icon on the security row says "Directory Password." Click that icon and you'll have the option to select a directory to open. By default the *Web Root* public directory should already be selected, so click the "Go" button.

You'll arrive on page that'll display all the file folders for your website. On this page you can select the folder you wish to "protect" by clicking on the file name. You can use this feature to require a username and password to access a folder or folders from the web. Some people use this feature to limit access to certain parts of their website.

Protecting a folder will protect <u>all folders</u> within that folder. Also, you will need to create users who can access the protected directory. You can give the password protected directory any name you want, no matter what the actual directory is called.

When a user accesses the protected directory through their web browser, they'll be prompted to enter a username and password. The name that you choose for the protected directory will appear as well. You can add and modify authorized users for any folders on your website. Just create a username and password for the person that needs to access the folder.

I used to see this feature used a lot 10 years ago because it was an easy way to create a membership website. Webmasters would "password protect" folders with pictures, video tutorials, and any other information they wanted to sell. After they collected payment, they would use this cPanel feature to create an authorized user that could access the protected folders.

I rarely see this method being used anymore. There are inexpensive **WordPress membership plugins** that'll allow users to access certain parts of your website depending on if they're a paid or free member. WordPress plugins will automate the process for you so you don't have to manually create authorized users for specific folders.

The next icon on the security row says "IP Deny Manager." Click that icon.

IP Deny Manager

The IP deny manager will allow you to block a range of IP addresses to prevent people from accessing your site. You can also enter a fully qualified domain name and the *IP Deny Manager* will attempt to resolve it to an IP address for you.

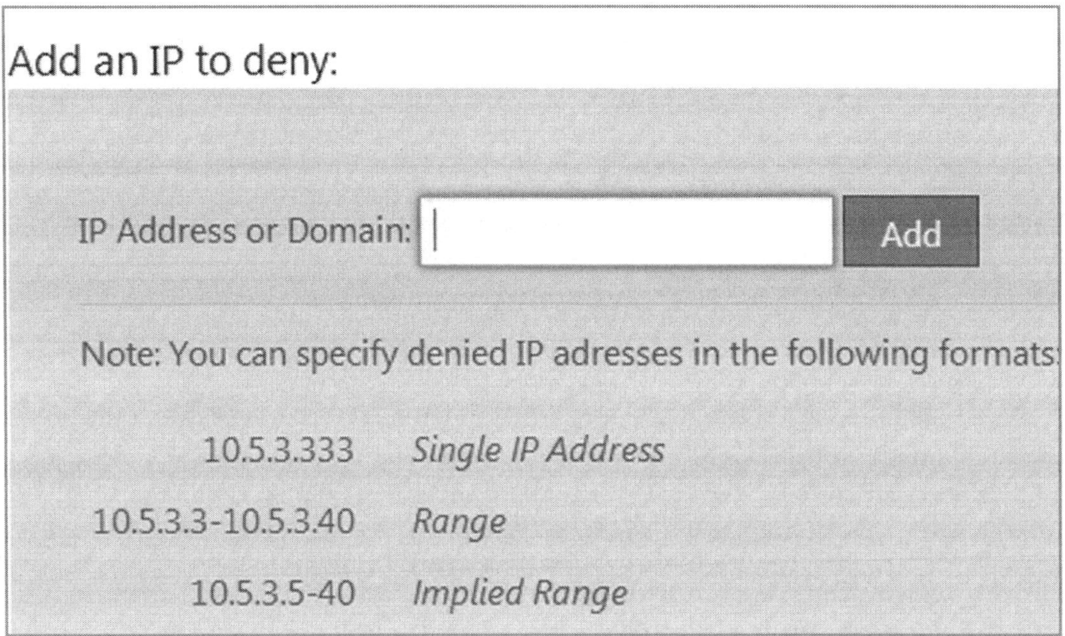

This page will also show a list of current IP addresses that are being blocked. You'll also have the option to remove the block on this same page.

I believe this is another feature that's obsolete with today's technology. There are **thousands** of free programs that you can use to scramble or change your IP address. Blocking someone from accessing your website by their IP address might stop a complete newbie, but that's about it.

If you decide to use the IP deny manager, you might block legitimate people that are trying to access your website. An internet troll that loves to start arguments on websites will find a way around the IP deny feature; but you can still try it!

The next icon says SSL/TLS Manager. Click on that icon.

SSL/TLS Manager

SSL stands for *Secure Socket Layer*. TLS stands for *Transport Layer Security*. Both SSL and TLS are protocols used to ensure traffic to and from your website are encrypted. This prevents 3rd parties from intercepting important personal data like credit card information.

You're going to need an SSL certificate if you plan on accepting credit card payments directly on your website. Most people won't submit personal information over the internet unless your website is secure. You also can't set up a merchant account if your website doesn't have an SSL certificate.

The SSL/TLS Manager icon will allow you to generate SSL certificates, signing requests, and keys. This is actually a complicated feature that your web host will set up for you. If you purchase a 3rd party SSL certificate and you know what you're doing, then you can upload your SSL certificate using this section.

If you really need an SSL certificate, I recommend purchasing one from your webhost instead of another 3rd party. After you web host sets everything up, you won't need to adjust anything within the SSL manager. You'll also have to purchase a dedicated IP address from your web host if you're going to use an SSL certificate.

The next item on the security row says SSH/Shell Access. Click that icon.

SSH/Shell Access

SSH keys will allow you to connect to a server, or multiple servers, without having to remember or enter your password for each system.

One immediate advantage this method has over traditional password authentication is that you can be authenticated by the server without ever having to send your password over the network. Anyone eavesdropping on your connection will not be able to intercept and crack your password because it is never actually transmitted.

This is an advanced feature that a basic WordPress user will never use. If you need a super secure way to transfer files, you can enable the security features with a stand-alone FTP client like Filezilla. If you're really tech savvy and you want to use SSH Access, you'll need to contact your web host.

The next icon says "Hotlink Protection." Click it.

Hotlink Protection

Hotlink protection prevents people from stealing bandwidth. An example of hotlinking would be using an image URL from your website to display your images somewhere else on the Web. The way someone could do this is by going to your images, right clicking, and then choosing the option that says "Copy Image URL."

Since a lot of web hosting companies offer unlimited bandwidth, this isn't as big a problem as it used to be. If someone really wants your image, they will just right click, choose "save image as" and save the image to their desktop. They can then host the image themselves without worry about you deleting the image. If you delete an image from your website, then whoever is "hotlinking" from you will lose the image too.

If you'd like to use the hotlink protection then click the "**Enable**" button. The Hotlink protection feature will let you add websites that are allowed to hotlink your images. You can enter all your websites into this section. You can also block access to certain extensions like jpg, jpeg, and png which are all image extensions.

Configure Hotlink Protection:

URLs to allow access:

```
http://blewhost.com
http://www.blewhost.com
```

Block direct access for these extensions (separate by commas):

```
jpg,jpeg,gif,png,bmp
```

Finally, you'll have the option to redirect people that aren't allowed to hotlink your images. You've probably noticed this before if you browse Google images a lot. Google images works by linking directly to your websites image URLS.

If the webmaster doesn't include Google as an allowed site, you'll get redirected somewhere else when you click to enlarge the image from Google. Other times you'll get redirected to a special page the webmaster created that says something sarcastic like, "*Nice try, better luck next time.*"

This is a nice feature, but it'll only prevent amateurs from stealing your images. If somebody really wants your image, they're going to get it by using the "save as" option or just simply taking a screenshot.

The next item on the list says "GnuPG Keys." Click that icon.

GnuPG Keys

The "GNU Privacy Guard", also known as *GnuPG* or *GPG*, is an open-source implementation for public-key cryptography. Public-key cryptography systems use public and private keys (keypairs) to encrypt and decrypt e-mail messages, files, and so on. Senders use recipients' public keys to encrypt items and recipients use their own private keys to decrypt the items.

Click the *GnuPG Keys* icon if you'd like to set this up. This is an advanced feature that you probably won't need, but it's very easy to set up. You should contact your web host if you need help setting up this feature.

Security Features for Go Daddy Users

Go Daddy's hosting control center has similar security features, but they don't have a "Security" section like cPanel. They do offer a **website protection scanner** for $6.99/month which offers some added protection to your website. You can read more about it here: http://www.godaddy.com/security/website-security.aspx

The site scanner does a few different things. The site scanner will:

- Give you a trusted site seal
- Daily malware link scan
- Daily website vulnerability scan
- Google "blacklist" check

The shared hosting plan with Go Daddy **does not** offer an IP Deny Manager, Hotlink Protection Manager, or GnuPG Keys. Most people don't use these tools anyway because they're advanced features that small to medium sized websites don't need. If you have a **VPS** or **Dedicated** hosting plan with Go Daddy, then your hosting plan with come with cPanel and you'll have these options available.

You also won't have access to an *SSL/TLS Manager* unless you purchase an SSL certificate. If you don't purchase an SSL certificate, then you don't need an SSL manager.

Password Protect Files

You can use Go Daddy to protect files using a directory password. To password protect files, just follow these steps:

- Click on your *File Manager* option
- Click the check box next to the folder that you want to protect
- Click the "Privacy" option on the top menu

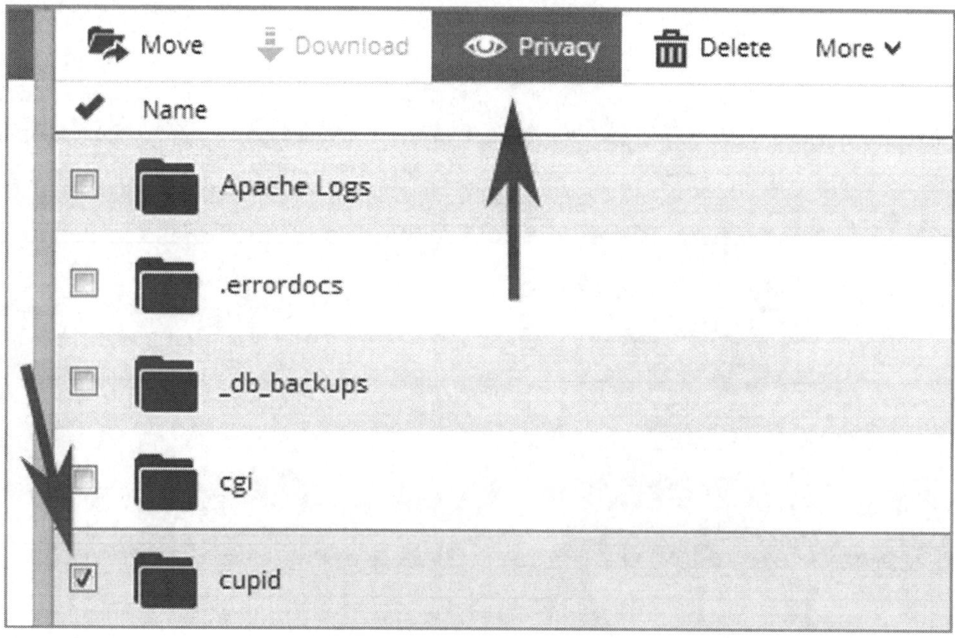

A window will open and you'll see 2 tabs. One tab will say "Permissions" and the other tab will say "Password." If you don't want the file to be visible to people browsing the web, then just un-check the box that says "Web Visible."

If you want to password protect the files then:

- Click the Password tab
- Click the "Password protect" check box
- Add users that are allowed to have access to the file

SSH Access

On your main dashboard you'll see an icon that says *SSH*. You can click that icon to create an SSH account. As I mentioned before, this is basically a very secure FTP client. You'll see a disclaimer telling you that you can use an FTP client to accomplish the same thing. All FTP clients will allow you to create a secure connection from your computer to your server.

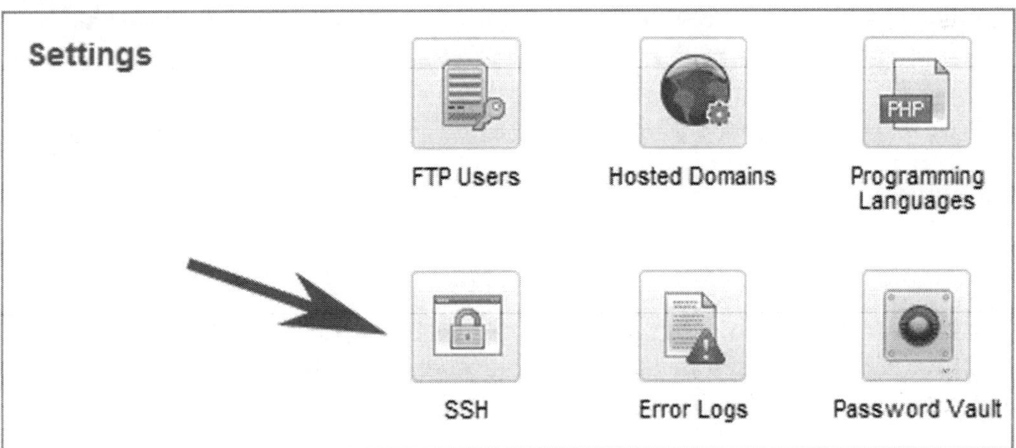

The SSH feature is a tool that would be used to send top secret confidential information. If you're not sending launch codes then it's probably a lot easier to use an FTP client. Since you're using WordPress, you probably won't need a stand-alone FTP client either, but it's up to you.

That covers the basic security setting if you're using Go Daddy. Let's move on to the next section where we'll talk about **Domain Management**.

Chapter 8

Domain Management

The domain management feature helps you organize, manage, and keep track of everything that has to do with your domain names. The first icon you'll see says "Domain Manager." Click that icon and you'll get forwarded to a page that has information regarding your purchased domain names and more.

Domain Manager

The domain manager will present you with a lot of options. You'll see an "Action Items" section that'll show you if you have any domain names that are due to expire. Below that you'll see a "Shortcuts" section that'll have clickable links that you can use to register a new domain name, transfer a domain and a few other options that are also available on your cPanel dashboard.

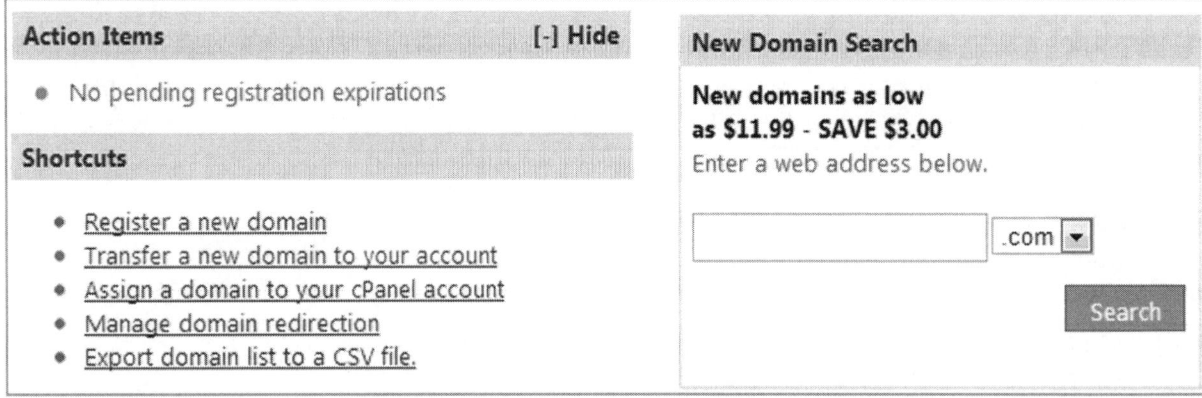

Below the "shortcuts" section you'll see another area with a list of your domain names. This section will show you when your domain name is due to expire and what type of domain name it is. If you click the check box next to your domain name, the box on the right side of the screen will display some information about the domain name such as:

- The domain registrar
- Name Servers (information needed to transfer your domain to/from another hosting provider)
- Transfer options

On the top right of this page you'll see a "New Domain Search" box. You can search for a new domain in that section if you want to start another website; or if you just want to reserve a new domain name for the future.

That covers everything for the "domain manager" icon. The next icon on the list will say "Register Domain."

Register Domain

After you click the *register domain* icon, you'll get forwarded to a page where you can search for a domain name. If the domain you want is available, you'll have the option to purchase it along with other extensions for that particular domain (.net, .org, .us, .info, .biz.) That's the only thing you can do on that page.

The next icon you'll see within your domain management options says "Transfer Domain." Click that icon.

Transfer Domain

This section will allow you to transfer a domain name you have with another registrar to your current hosting provider. Just enter the domain name you want to transfer and follow the step-by-step process.

Transfer - Select a Domain

Enter domain to transfer: [ ] Continue

If you need additional help, there's a link to a video on the page showing you how to transfer your domain. If you're still confused, then contact customer support and they'll be happy to assist you.

If you plan on transferring a domain name, **don't wait** until the last minute. Some registrars will *LOCK* the domain when it approaches close to the expiration date. This prevents the domain from being able to be transferred away from them.

The time from now until your current expiration date will be transferred for FREE, so you will not lose anything you've already paid for. Since you don't lose anything by transferring, you should transfer a domain name sooner rather than later to avoid complications.

The next icon you'll see within the domain management section will say "Subdomains." Click the sub-domain icon.

Sub-Domains

If your website was **bluehost.com**, a sub-domain would be **blog.bluehost.com.** A sub-domain can act as if it's an entirely different website, or it can be used as a shortcut to another place on your website. For example, *maps.google.com* is a shortcut to get to "Google Maps" faster.

To create a sub-domain, just type the sub-domain you want in the field next to your domain name and click "create." If you were to create a sub-domain like blog.bluehost.com, then by default your web host will attempt to load pages found inside the directory "blog" within your *public_html* directory. In a situation like this, you don't need to add a redirect to your sub-domain.

Create a Subdomain

Subdomain: . blewhost.com

Home folder (aka Document Root) for your subdomain: /public_html/

Create

If you want your sub-domain to redirect to different location, you can select the directory before you click the "create" button or manually create a "redirect." I'll show you how to manually create a redirect later.

It may take a few hours before everyone on the internet can access your new sub-domain because the domain name service (DNS) will need to be updated. Some web hosting providers will make it possible to access the new sub-domain almost immediately.

If you want to create an entirely different website on your sub-domain, then you'll need to use the Add-on feature which I'll go over shortly. When in doubt, just contact your web host and let them know what you're trying to do. Tech support will help get you set up within a few minutes and you can write down the steps for future reference.

The next icon within the domain management section says "Addon Domains." Click that icon to set up add-on domains.

Add-on Domains

Add-on domains are top-level domains that point to a sub-directory in your current web hosting account. In simple terms, you can create multiple websites one a single hosting account by using the "Add-on" domain feature.

You can use this feature to create a completely separate website for yourself, a friend, or a family member. That's why it's important to choose a hosting package that offers unlimited domain hosting so you can host more than one website on the same hosting account.

Usually the cheapest hosting package will only allow you to host one domain name, so it's not possible to use the add-on domain feature. Look for a web hosting package that will allow you to host multiple websites on a single hosting plan.

After you click the "Addon Domains" icon, you'll get forwarded to a page that will help you assign your domain name to your hosting account. You need to purchase the domain name you want **FIRST** before you can use the add-on feature.

Step 1: Enter Domain

First, select a domain name that you would like to assign.

Use a domain that is already associated with your account.

Domain: All domains assigned

OR

Use a domain that is **not** already associated with your account.

Domain:

If you purchased the domain name with your current hosting provider, then the domain name you're looking for will show up in a drop-down list. If you want to use a domain name that you purchased from another registrar, then you'll see a box where you can manually enter the domain name. If it's a 3rd party domain, you'll have to go through a verification process first before your hosting account will allow you to add the new domain.

Next you'll have to choose how you would like to assign the domain. You'll have the option to assign the domain as an:

- **Addon Domain**: An Add-on Domain is a domain name that points to a different subdirectory on your account. This gives you the ability to make it look like an entirely different website
- **Parked Domain**: A Parked Domain (or pointed domain) is a domain name that points to the same directory as your Primary domain.
- **Unassigned Domain**: An Unassigned Domain is attached to your account, but does not point to a website or have a dedicated folder attached. When you're ready to host this domain on your account, this tool can help you make it an *Add-on* or *Parked* domain.

Select "Addon Domain" and move on to the next section. The next section will ask you to specify a directory that you'd like the add-on domain to point too. You'll have the option to use an existing directory or **have cPanel create a new directory for you**. Since you want to create a new website, select the option that says "Create a new directory."

A sub-domain is required for your add-on domain because it's actually an extension of your main domain. For the sud-domain field, just enter the name of your website.

For example, if the main domain name for your hosting account were *bluehost.com* and your add-on domain was *matthewpitt.com;* then you should enter *matthewpitt* into the sub-domain field. So the entire sub-domain should look like this: **matthewpitt.bluehost.com.**

People will be able to access your website 2 different ways. They could go straight to **matthewpitt.com** or use the sub-domain **matthewpitt.bluehost.com.** When you're finish, click the "Assign this domain" button. After your add-on domain is created, you can install WordPress onto that domain name and start creating a new website.

Your add-on domains will share the disk space and bandwidth limitations with your main domain. If you have a hosting account that offers unlimited disk space, unlimited bandwidth, and unlimited databases, then you can create unlimited WordPress websites on a single hosting account.

The next icon on the domain management section says "Parked Domains." Click that icon and you'll arrive back at the same page as the "add-on domains" page.

Parked Domains

As mentioned earlier, a "Parked Domain" is a domain name that points to the same directory as your primary domain. This means that the website on the parked domain will be the same as your primary domain. This page looks exactly like the "add-on domains" page. The only difference is that the "Parked Domain" box is checked by default this time.

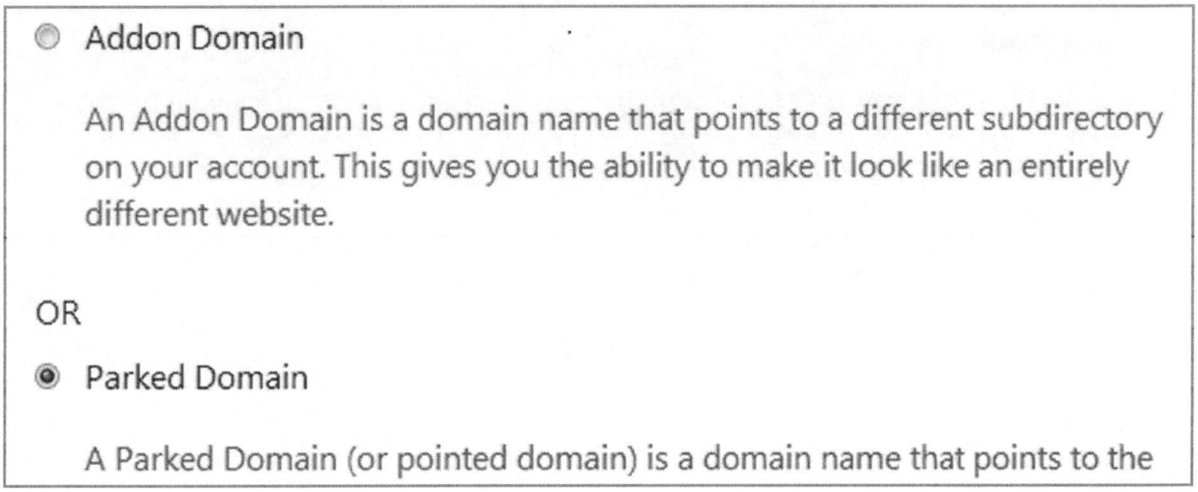

Addon Domain

An Addon Domain is a domain name that points to a different subdirectory on your account. This gives you the ability to make it look like an entirely different website.

OR

Parked Domain

A Parked Domain (or pointed domain) is a domain name that points to the

Some business owners will buy a domain name along with all of its major extensions. Using *Bluehost* as an example, the owners could protect their brand from imposters by purchasing bluehost.com, bluehost.net, bluehost.org, and bluehost.info. After they purchase all the extensions, they could assign the extensions their not using as *parked* domains.

Another good way to protect your brand is to use the *redirect* feature. You can buy the most popular extensions associated with your domain name and redirect those domain names to your primary domain. You can do this by clicking the next icon on the domain management row that says "Redirects."

Redirects

Redirects are exactly what they sound like. You can redirect one URL to another URL using this feature. You could use a redirect for a long URL in favor of a shorter and easier to remember URL. You can also purchase different extensions of your domain name and common misspellings and redirect them to your main website.

Choose the domain name from the drop-down menu that you'd like to redirect. In the next box, manually enter the website that you'd like the assigned URL to be redirected too.

Add Redirect

A permanent redirect will notify the visitor's browser to update any boo redirected. Temporary redirects will not update the visitor's bookmarks.

Permanent (301) Temporary (302)

http://(www.)? ** All Public Domains ** /

redirects to →

http://

You'll also see an option that says **Permanent (301)** and **Temporary (302)**. A *301 redirect* will tell search engines that the redirect is permanent, and they should update their records and stop linking to the old URL for that source.

A *302 redirect* tells the search engines that the redirect is temporary and the search engine does nothing. It doesn't matter to the end users; either way they're going to get redirected.

The next icon on the domain management sections says "DNS Zone Editor." Click that icon.

DNS Zone Editor

This is an advanced feature that you don't need to bother with. If you don't have experience using a DNS zone editor, then leave everything as it is. DNS is the component of the internet which converts human-readable domain names (such as *bluehost.com*) into computer-readable IP addresses (*such as 192.0.32.10*).

It does this according to "DNS zone files" that reside on your server and tie domain names to IP addresses. There are several different types of records in a domain's zone file. This feature allows you to create, edit, and delete *A*, *CNAME*, and *TXT* records.

If this seems confusing, that's because it is. Leave this section alone. Your WordPress website will function fine without you editing this section. If anything needs to be changed within the DNS zone editor, tech support will do this for you.

The next item says "CloudFlare" which is a bonus feature that you may or may not see depending on your web host. Click that icon.

CloudFlare

CloudFlare is a free and paid add-on feature that'll help speed up your website and add security features. The free version works just fine, but the paid version has some added features that you might find useful. The paid version of CloudFlare is $14.99 per domain name.

The reason you'll see this feature in your domain management section is because you'll have to add *CloudFlare* to each domain separately. If you have any problems using this feature, then read all the documentation or just contact your web host. For more information about *CloudFlare*, you can visit their overview page at: https://www.cloudflare.com/overview.

Go Daddy Domain Management

Go Daddy has way more management features compared to *Bluehost* and most other web hosting providers. Because of the wide variety of features, Go Daddy's domain dashboard is a bit more complicated compared to cPanel. I'll show you how to navigate your dashboard to accomplish the same tasks as cPanel.

Register a New Domain Name

To register a domain name is really simple. After you log into you hosting account, just click the link on the top menu that says "Find Your Domain." After you click that link you'll get forwarded to a page where you can search for a new domain name.

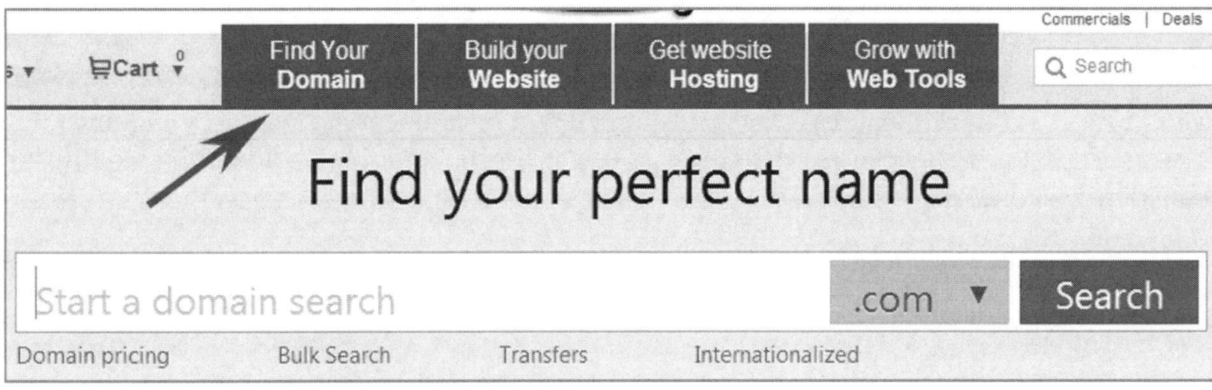

You can use the drop-down menu to choose which extension you're looking for. Go Daddy has a lot of extensions compared to other web hosting providers. You'll see extensions such as **.co**, **.me**, **.tv**, **.com.au**, **.asia**, **.eu**, **.fr**, **.co.uk**, and a lot more.

After you pick the extension you're looking for, just click the search button to see if the domain name is available. If the domain you want is available and you want it, then purchase it and the domain name will automatically get added to your account.

Transfer Domain

To transfer a domain name, simply follow the same steps as if you were going to purchase a domain name. Click the "Find Your Domain" link on the top menu and you'll get forwarded to the screen to search for domain names.

You'll notice a link under the search box that says "transfers." Click that link and you'll get forwarded to another screen that prompts you to enter the domain name you want to transfer. Follow the steps on that page to transfer your domain name to Go Daddy.

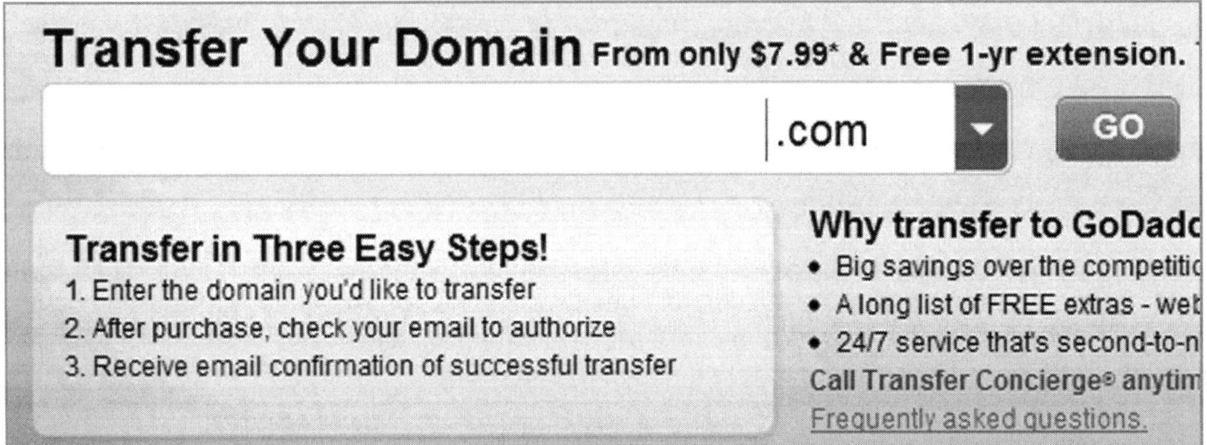

Don't forget that when you transfer your domain to a new provider; you'll have to pay for a 1 year extension with the new web host. If you need help, just contact Go Daddy for assistance.

Sub-Domains

To create a sub-domain; click the "launch" button that's on the web hosting section of your dashboard and follow the steps below:

- From the "More" menu, select the *Hosted Domains* option.

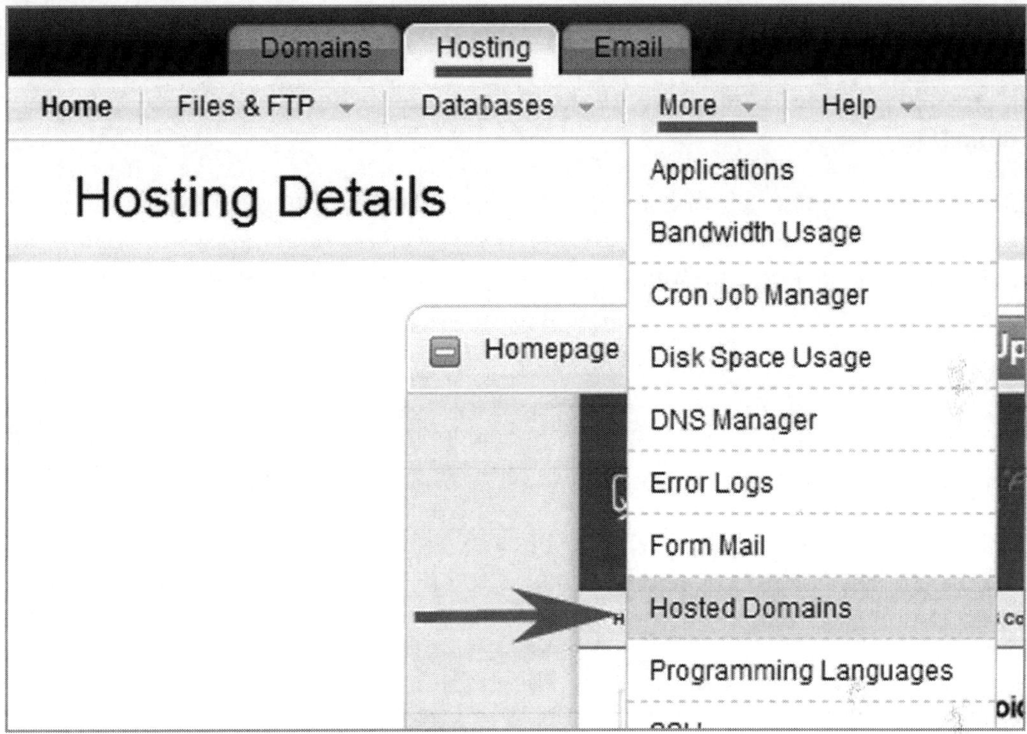

- In the Domain Name column, click the domain name you want to use. (click on the actual domain name, not the check box next to it.)
- Click "Add Sub-domain."
- Enter a single sub-domain or multiple sub-domains separated by a comma.
- Select whether the sub-domain content will reside in a folder of the <u>same name</u> or a <u>new</u> or <u>existing folder</u>.
- Click "Ok."

Add-on Domains

To use the add-on domain feature, make sure that you've already purchased the domain name first. After you have the domain name you want to use for your new website, follow these steps:

- Click "launch" on the web hosting section of your hosting control center.
- From the "More" menu, select *Hosted Domains.*
- Click the "Add Domain" button on the top right.
- Enter the domain name you want to add, and enter a name for the "folder" section. This new folder will enable to you to create completely new website for this domain name. Ideally, you should name the folder the same name as your new domain name. This will help you easily identify the folder when you're using your file manager.
- Click the "OK" button, and you'll see an alert that says "pending set-up." It should only take about 15-30 minutes for your new domain to get set up. You can now install WordPress on the domain name and create a new website for your friends, family, or yourself.

Parked Domains

Parked Domains are different with Go Daddy. Parked domains are domains that display a temporary web page when someone enters your domain name in a Web browser.

If you host a domain name with Go Daddy but never build a website on that domain name, it'll automatically turn into a parked domain. You'll just see a web page with a lot of Go Daddy advertisements on it.

If you don't plan on creating a website on a particular domain anytime soon, you can enroll that domain name into a program called **CashParking**. CashParking is a service that allows you to earn money on your parked domain name.

If you associate your domains with your *CashParking* account, Go Daddy's advertising partners will place context-relevant advertisements on your page. Each time a visitor clicks on a displayed advertisement, you'll receive a share of the generated click-through revenue based on your CashParking plan. The amount you receive and the price you pay for the CashParking service depends on the plan you select.

You can add an **unlimited** number of domains to your CashParking account. To enroll into CashParking, click the "launch" button on the **domain section** of your dashboard. You'll get forwarded to another screen that'll list all your domain names. From that screen you can either click the check box next to the domain that you want to manage, or click on the domain name directly.

For simplicity sake, just click on the domain name that you want to manage. On the next screen you'll see a menu item that says "Buy & Sell." There you'll find a drop down menu that says "Add CashParking."

You can learn more about CashParking by clicking that link, and then you can decide if you want to purchase the service or not. If you have additional questions, just contact Go Daddy.

Redirects

To set up a redirect you'll need to click the launch button on the domain section of your dashboard. Click on the domain name that you want to set up with a redirect.

If you scroll about half way down the page, you'll see a setting that says "Fowarding." Within that section you'll see a link that says "Manage" for domains and sub-domains. Click the "manage" link and you'll have the option to add a forward/redirect for that domain name.

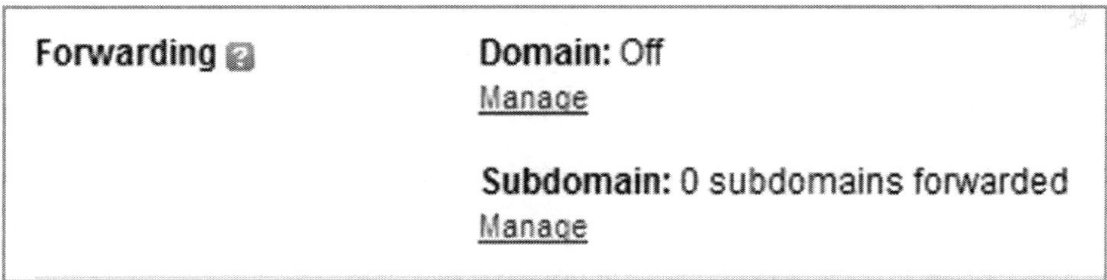

Just like Bluehost, you'll just have to enter in the web address you want your domain name to get forward too. You can also choose if this will be a *301 Permanent* or a *302 Temporary* redirect. Go Daddy also has a "masking" feature that might come in handy if you're an affiliate marketer.

The masking feature will redirect a user to the new URL but display the original URL in the browser. So this feature will "mask" or hide the web address that you just redirected the person too.

DNS Zone Editor

As mentioned earlier, this is an advanced feature so I don't recommend changing anything unless you know what you're doing. To find the *DNS Zone Editor* you'll have to click the "launch" button on the web hosting section of your dashboard. You'll see an icon on this page that says "DNS Manager." Click that link to edit or make changes to your DNS zone.

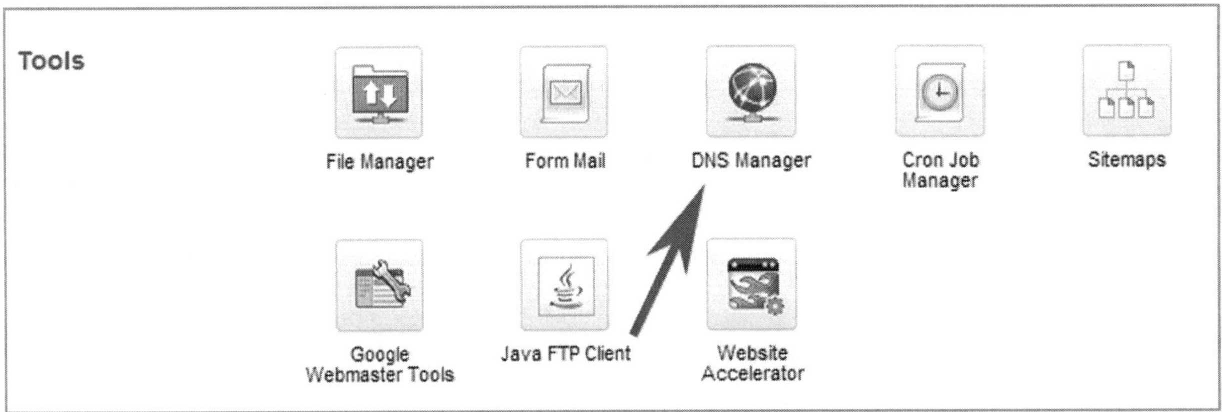

Bonus Features

You can use Go Daddy's domain manager to perform a lot of actions. You'll see most of these options by clicking the "launch" button on the domain section of your dashboard. If you click on your domain name, you'll get forwarded to a page that has a top menu that will allow you to:

- Manage auto renewals
- Renew your domain
- Upgrade your domain with added features: Privacy, Protected Registration, Certified Domain, SSL Certificates, and Business Registration for your domain name.
- Sell on "premium listings"
- List your domain on Go Daddy's auction
- Get a domain appraisal
- Transfer the domain over to someone else
- Run a diagnostics on your domain name
- Delete your domain name

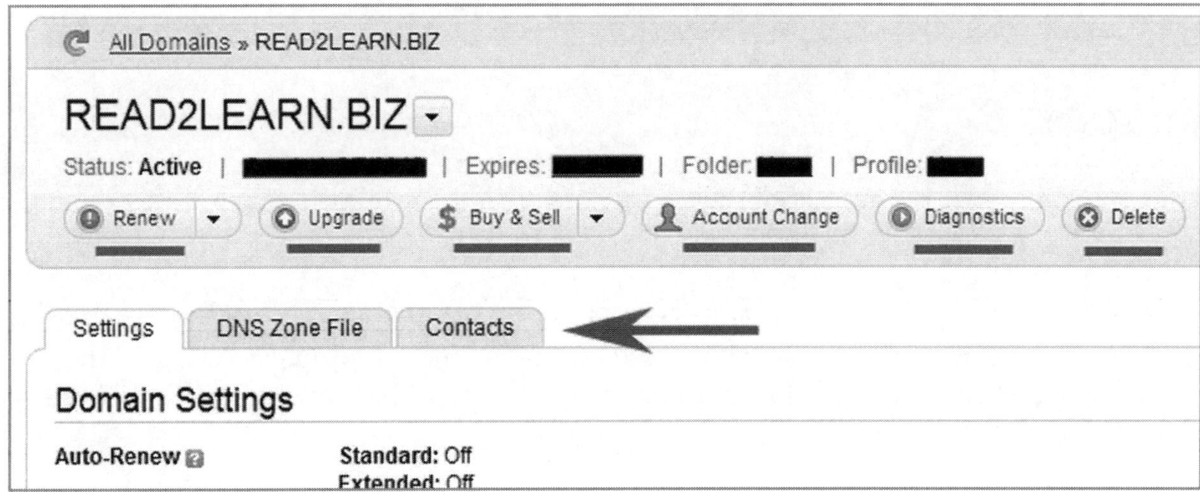

Below that you'll see 3 tabs:

<u>Settings</u>: This tab will allow you to change the settings on your domain name such as forwarding, auto-renew, domain locking, and name-server info.

<u>DNS Zone File</u>: Zone files organize the zone records for domain names and sub-domains in a DNS server. Every domain name and sub-domain has a zone file, and each zone file contains zone records.

These files, editable in any plain text editor, hold the DNS information linking domain names and sub-domains to IP addresses. Zone files usually contain several different zone records.

<u>Contacts</u>: The *Internet Corporation for Assigned Names and Numbers* (ICANN), the governing body for domain names, requires valid contact information (registrant, technical, billing, and administrative). If you enter false information, your domain name can be canceled.

This section will show your contact information that's on file in the "WHOIS" database. If you want to protect your personal information, make sure that you purchase the **domain privacy** add-on when you buy your domain name.

If you purchase the domain privacy feature, you won't see your private information in this section. Instead you'll see the contact information for *Domains By Proxy, LLC* which is the company that keeps your domain registration private.

That covers everything within Go Daddy's domain manager. In the next chapter I'll give you a brief overview of databases, what they're used for, and how to create new databases.

Chapter 9

Database Tools

cPanel offers simple tools that'll allow you to work with databases. WordPress is a web script, and web scripts require at least one database to function properly. The good news is that the "one-click install" feature automatically creates a database for you when install WordPress.

As a WordPress user you'll probably never have to manually create a database. If the circumstance arises when you have to manually create a database, add users to a database, or delete a database, then you'll need to use the "database tools" feature within cPanel.

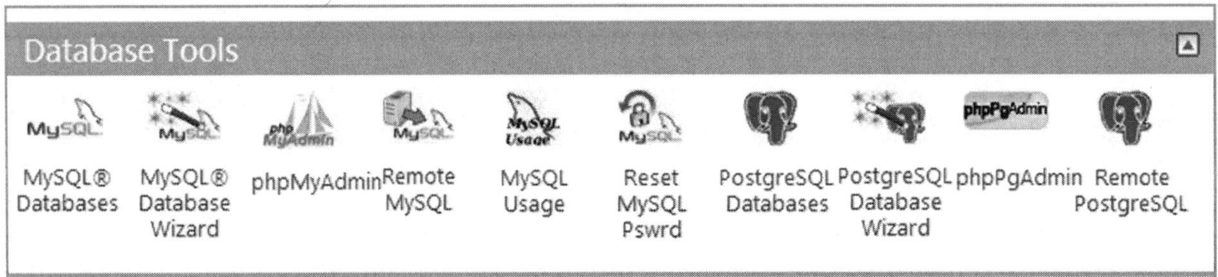

If you look at the *Database Tools* section within cPanel, you'll notice that there are 2 types of databases:

- MySQL Databases
- PostgreSQL Databases

Both *MySQL* and *Postgre* perform the same tasks, but they do it differently. WordPress uses MySQL so I'm only going to focus on that feature. Some web hosts will only provide you with MySQL database tools because it's the most popular with the most support. Click the first icon that says "MySQL Databases" to create a database. Manually creating a database is a 3 step process:

1. Create a New Database - name your database and click on the "create database button"
2. Add New User – Before you can use the database, you'll need to add at least one user.

3. Add User to Database – You'll need to associate the *user* with the *database*. You'll see a drop-down menu where you can choose the *user* and the *database* that you want to associate together.

It's important to note that you can add a single user to multiple databases. So if you need to create a new database in the future, you can associate the user you previously created to the new database.

After you associate the user with the database, you'll see the new database under the "Current Databases" section. There you'll also see information about the size of the database, users, an option to delete the user, and an option to delete the database. Deleting the user only removes the user from that database.

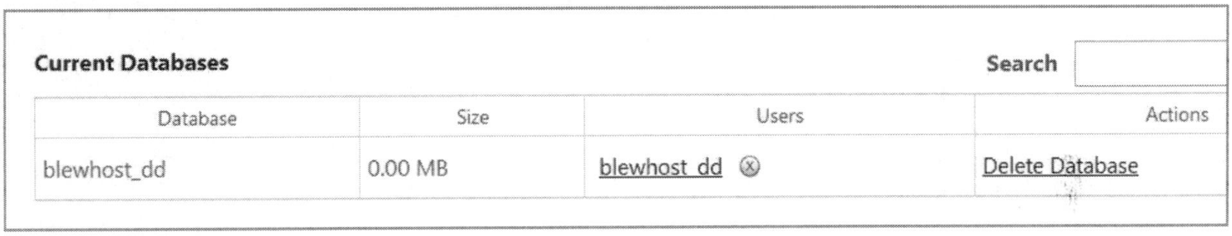

Current Databases Search

Database	Size	Users	Actions
blewhost_dd	0.00 MB	blewhost_dd ⊗	Delete Database

If you'd like to completely delete the user from all active databases, then you'll have to scroll all the way down the screen. You'll see a section that says "Current Users" that'll list all the current database users. This is where you can delete a user from having access to **all** active databases.

You can check your database for problems by clicking the "*Check DB*" button on the screen. If there are any errors, then click the "*Repair DB*" button which you'll see on the same screen.

MySQL Database Wizard

The next icon on the list says MySQL Database Wizard. You can create a new database using this wizard feature if you need an easier solution.

The database wizard will give you a step-by-step guide to create a new database. You'll only have to enter a small piece of information into each screen and then click the "Next Step" button. By the time you arrive to the last screen you'll have a database created.

phpMyAdmin

The "phpMyAdmin" icon will allow you add, remove, backup and restore data in the databases you've created. This is a very advanced tool, and the chances of you ever using this tool are about 1%. There are entire books dedicated to learning *phpMyAdmin* because it's a very complex tool. I'll explain the main interface for you since you may need to access this tool at some point.

If you click the *phpMyAdmin* icon, you'll get forwarded to a page that'll ask you for your username and password. They're asking you for the username and password for the database user that you've created. If you've manually created a database user, then you should have all this information handy or saved somewhere.

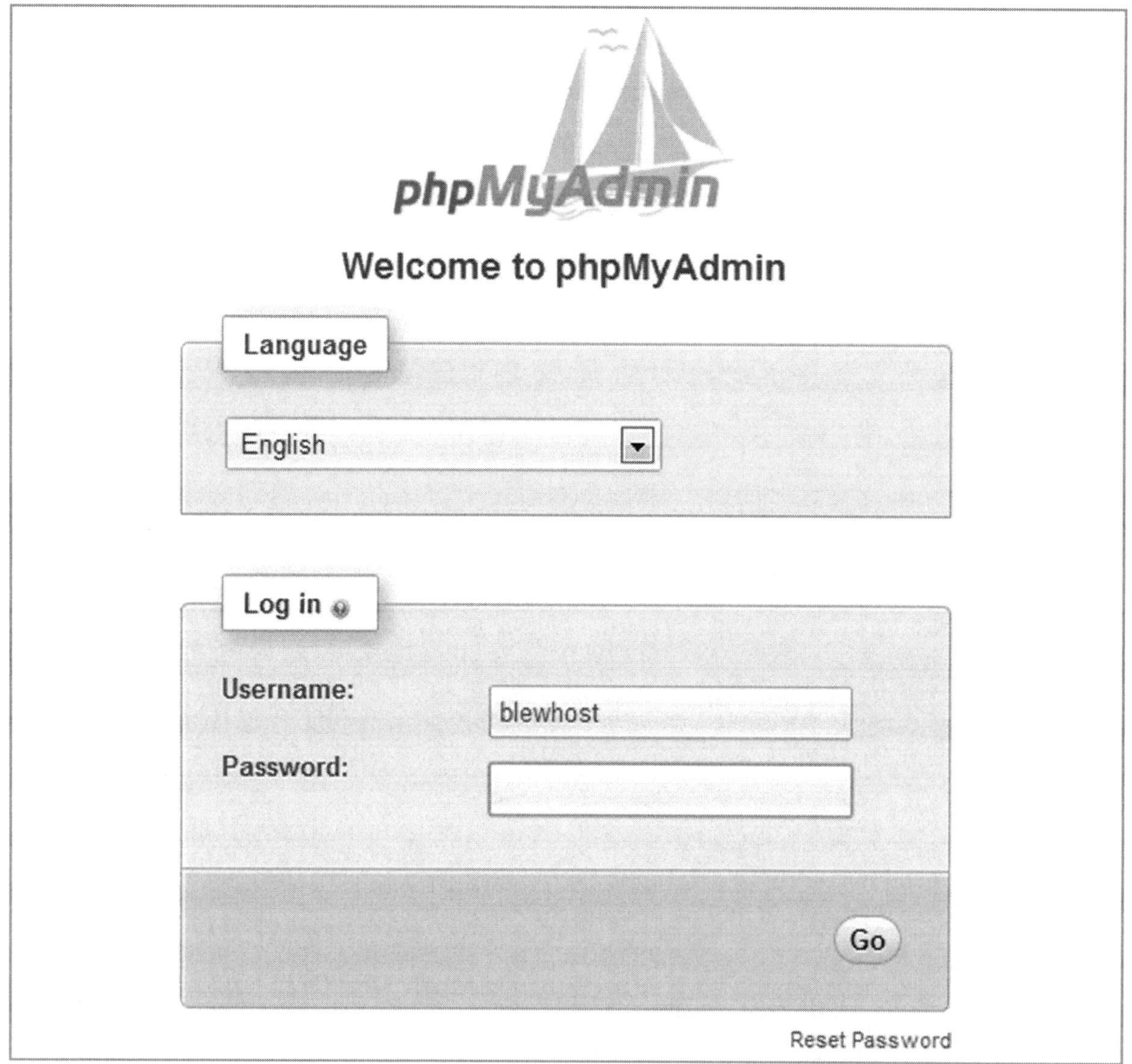

If you used the WordPress "one-click" install feature when you created your website, then your hosting provider automatically created a database for you. To find your username for the database, go back to the *MySQL Database* section within cPanel and you'll see your database username there.

The WordPress "one-click" install feature automatically created a password for your database as well. On the main *phpMyAdmin* screen you'll have the option to click a link that'll allow you to reset your password.

If you decide to change your password, PLEASE BE AWARE that any WordPress scripts that are using the old password will **not** be automatically updated. These applications will break until you update them to use the new password.

If you'd like to retrieve the database password that was automatically created for you instead, follow these steps:

- Navigate to the "File Management" area of your cPanel dashboard
- Click the "File Manager" icon
- Make sure the "Web Root" option is checked and click the *GO* button
- On the next screen, look for a file that says **wp-config.php**, click on the file, and then click the "Edit" button on the toolbar

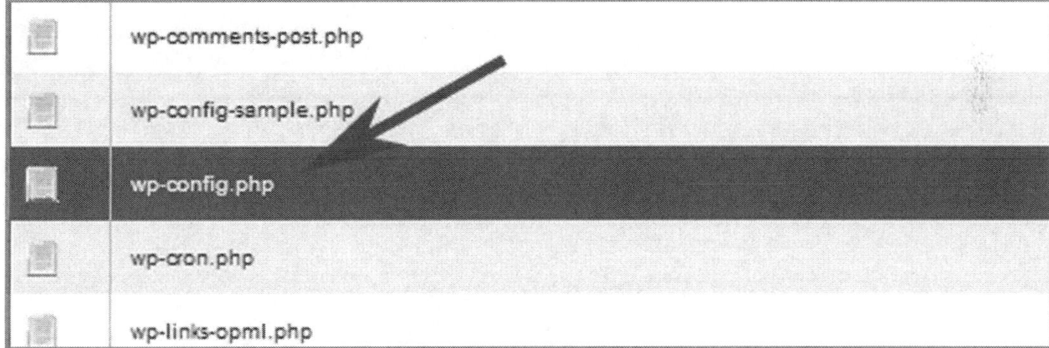

- A pop-up box will appear, and you need to click the "edit" button on the pop-up box
- You'll get forwarded to a text file that will display your MySQL database <u>username</u> and <u>password</u>

```
/** MySQL database username */
define('DB_USER', '[illegible]d1');

/** MySQL database password */
define('DB_PASSWORD', '[illegible]b9');

/** MySQL hostname */
define('DB_HOST', 'localhost');

/** Database Charset to use in creating database tables. */
define('DB_CHARSET', 'utf8');
```

After you retrieve your username and password, you'll be able to sign into phpMyAdmin. Sign in and you'll notice that the main screen is divided into two sections. On the left side of the screen you'll see the database sidebar. On the right of the screen you'll see the main interface. Within the main interface you'll see small "question marks" that'll link to documentation that will explain each feature.

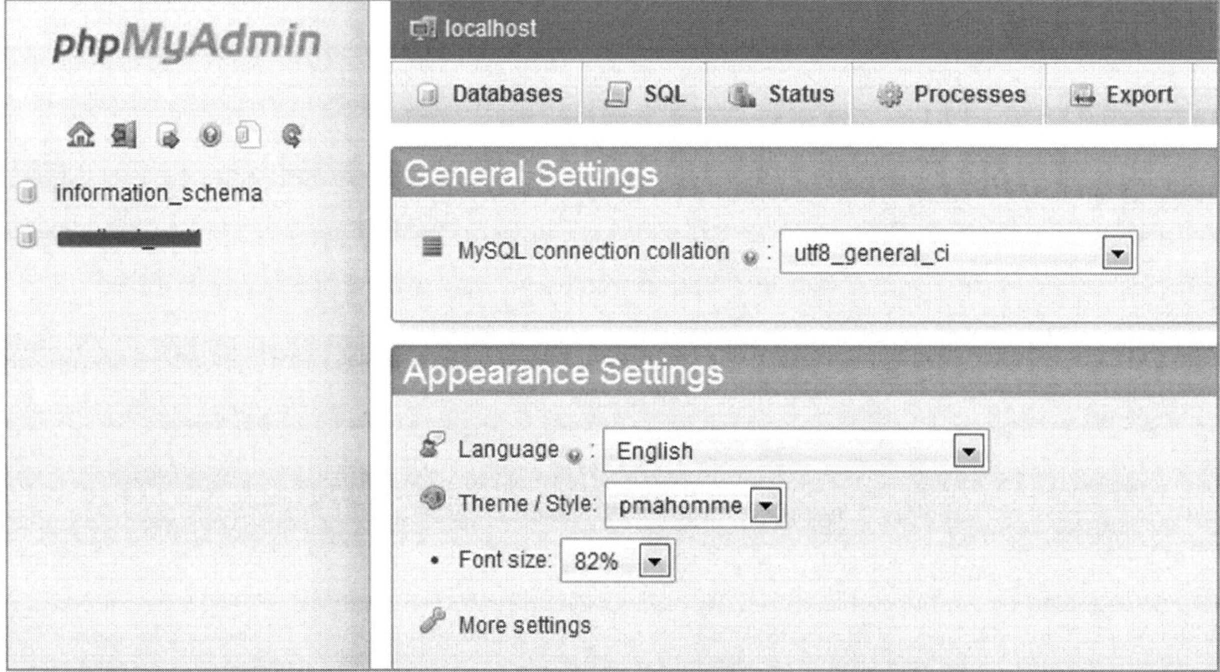

The left sidebar will allow you to select a database to work with by clicking on it. After you select a database, all of the main database categories will be listed. Clicking on a category will show you all the data for that category on the main screen. You can add, delete, or edit data using that screen.

You can also **backup your database** by clicking the "Export" tab at the top. The default settings on the "export" screen should be fine. Click the "save as" box at the bottom of the screen, and press the "go" button.

If you want to backup your database, I recommend using the "Site Backup Pro" feature mentioned earlier in this book. You'll find that feature within the "File Management" section of your cPanel.

Remote MySQL

The next icon you'll see will say Remote MySQL. This is another advanced feature that allows you to add an access host. You have the option to submit an *IP* or *Class C* to setup the remote MySQL grant rules and also to allow access through the firewall.

As a new WordPress user, there's no reason for you to manually create or edit database information. If you do need to access database information, simply use the basic *phpMyAdmin* method.

MySQL Usage

The *MySQL* icon will give you some basic information about your databases. You'll see how many databases you have along with detailed information about how much disk space it's using.

Reset MySQL Pswrd

Click this icon if you want to reset your database password to your **main** account. If you just want to update or change your password to individual accounts, then you can do that by clicking the "MySQL Database" icon within cPanel. Scroll all the way down the screen and you'll see a list of database users. Click on the user that has a password that you'd like to update. You'll have to know the previous password to change the password using this option.

Other Database Tools

You'll notice other database tools for **PostgreSQL**. WordPress uses MySQL, so I'm not going to go into details about PostgreSQL. If you take a quick glance, you'll notice that the options for PostgreSQL are the same as MySQL.

If you need to create or delete a PostgreSQL database, just use the PostgreSQL icons the same way you would use MySQL. Also instead of using *phpMyAdmin*, you'll notice that PostgreSQL uses something called *phpPgAdmin*. Depending on your web host you might not even see anything for PostgreSQL; but all web hosts will have MySQL management tools.

Go Daddy Database Tools

To access your database tools using Go Daddy, click the launch button on the web hosting section. At the bottom of the screen you'll see the *MySQL* icon. Click the *MySQL* icon to manage your databases.

After you click the icon, you'll get forwarded to a screen that'll display all of your active databases. On the top left you'll see a button that says "Add." Click that button if you want to manually create a database.

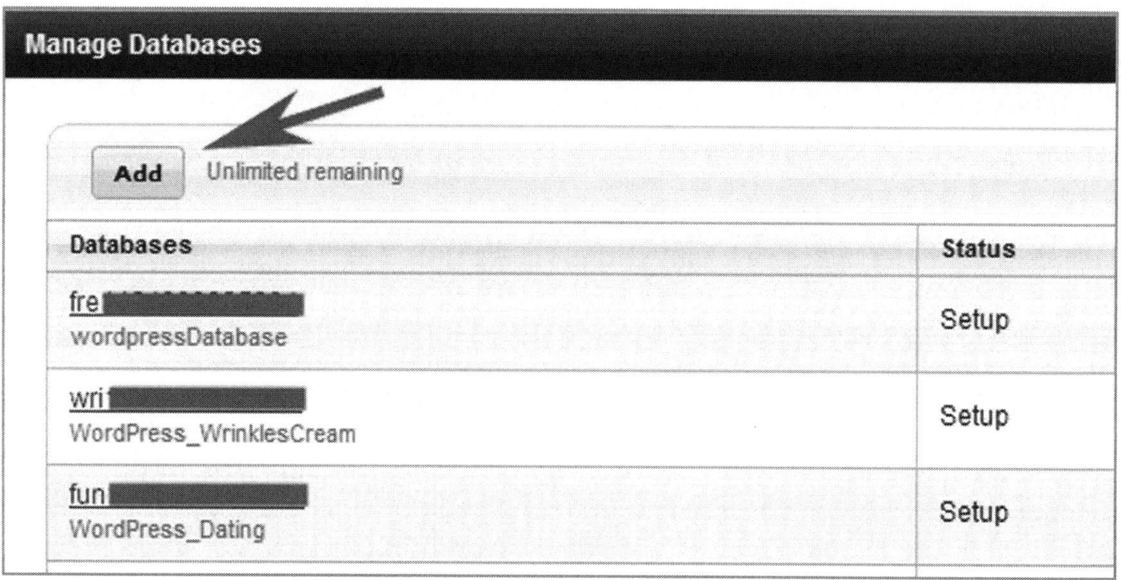

Next to your active databases you'll see a drop-down button that says "**Actions**." You can use this button to:

- View database details
- Back Up your database
- Restore your database
- Delete your database

Next to the "Actions" button you'll see another button that says **phpMyAdmin**. Click that button and you'll get forwarded to a screen that'll ask you for your username and password for the database.

Go Daddy has the WordPress "one-click install" feature too, so that means your username and password was automatically generated. You'll see your usernames on the database management screen. If you want to find your current password, you can look it up in your file manager the same way I mentioned earlier:

- Click on your file manager
- Click directly on the **wp-config.php** link
- Another screen will open that will display your database username and password

If you want to reset your password, click on the "Actions" button from the database management screen. From that drop-down menu click on the "details" option and you'll see a section that'll allow you to reset your password.

That's all you need to know about databases if you're a WordPress user. I'm almost certain that you'll never need to change or edit anything with your databases. I've played around with phpMyAdmin few times to learn how to manually back-up a database, but it's not necessary.

If you create multiple WordPress websites and decide to let some of those domains expire; you can use the database management feature to delete the assigned database as well. Just because you let a domain name expire doesn't mean that your hosted files suddenly disappear too.

You'll have to manually delete the files from your server if you're completely done with an old website. The only way you'll only lose your website files is if your hosting account expires and you don't reinstate your account within the specified grace period.

That covers everything you'll need to know about databases. In the next chapter we'll briefly go over a few advanced "Software/Service" features within your cPanel dashboard.

Chapter 10

Software/Services

The **software/services** section of cPanel contains mostly advanced features for web developers. The only feature within this section that you might use is the first icon that says "CGI Center."

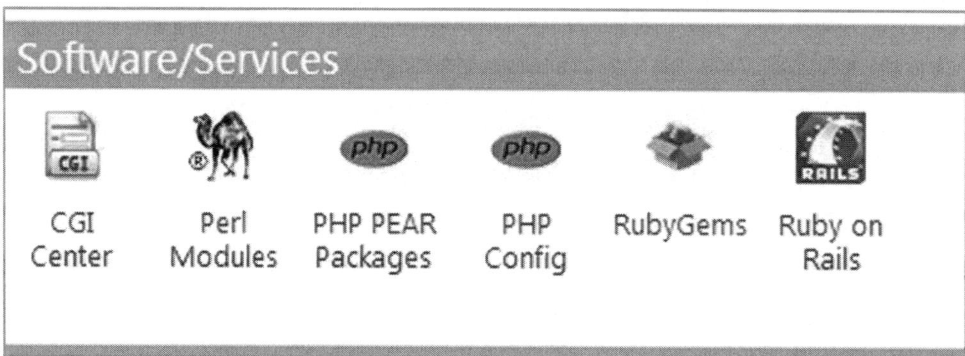

CGI Center

The CGI center contains widgets that you can add to your website. Some of the widgets included are:

- Counter – create a counter that displays how many visitors have been to your site.
- Clock – This utility will create a real-time Java clock on your website.
- Countdown – Create a display that counts down to a specific date.

There are a lot more features too. Look through all the options and decide if you see something that catches your attention. You can choose your settings for these widgets, and then cPanel will generate a *HTML* code that you can paste on your website.

To use the *HTML* code on your WordPress website, you'll have to use a "text" widget. If you're familiar with WordPress widgets, then you know that you can paste *HTML* code into the *text* widget.

Perl Modules

The "Perl Modules" icon will redirect you to a page that'll allow you to install a Perl Module. Perl Modules are collections of functions that allow you to perform tasks in *Perl*. As a WordPress user, you'll never need to install a Perl Module.

If you'd like to learn more about Perl Modules, you can check out these two links:

- http://en.wikipedia.org/wiki/Perl_module
- http://learnperl.scratchcomputing.com/tutorials/modules/

PHP PEAR Packages

The "PHP PEAR Packages" icon will redirect you to a page that will allow you to install a PEAR package. PEAR packages are collections of functions that allow you to perform tasks in PHP.

This is another section within cPanel that isn't necessary for WordPress users. If you'd like to learn more about PHP PEAR Packages, then you can check out these two links:

- http://en.wikipedia.org/wiki/PEAR
- http://pear.php.net/

PHP Config

After you click the PHP Config icon, you'll get forwarded to a page where you can change which version of PHP you're using. You'll see a disclaimer warning you that if you're not familiar with these options, *do NOT change them.* If you misconfigure your PHP settings, this will cause all PHP scripts on your site to stop functioning.

Ruby Gems

The Ruby Gems icon will forward to a page where you can install a "Gem" to use within Ruby. Ruby Gems are collections of functions that allow you to perform tasks in Ruby.

If you'd like to learn more about Ruby Gems, you can check out these two links:

- http://en.wikipedia.org/wiki/RubyGems
- http://docs.rubygems.org/read/book/1

Ruby on Rails

The last icon within the *Software/Service* section of cPanel says Ruby on Rails. Since you're a beginner, the chances of you creating a "Rails" application are slim to none.

If you do plan on creating a "Rails" application, then Bluehost has a tutorial to help you set everything up correctly. You can find the documentations by following this link: https://my.bluehost.com/cgi/help/207

As you may have noticed, most of the icons within the *Software/Services* sections are highly advanced features. I would've skipped this section, but I wanted to at least give you some reference links to find out more information if you're interested to learn more. Your WordPress website will function perfectly without you changing any of these advanced options.

The next section under the "Software/Services" area says "Advanced." This section of cPanel will have more advanced features that you might not use. I'll briefly go over the icons within this *advanced* section along with some useful links for more information.

Advanced

The First icon you'll see will say **Apache Handlers**. Apache handlers control how the apache web server software manages certain file types and extensions for your site.

You can configure apache to handle a new file type with an existing handler by manually adding a new handler. If you'd like to learn more about *Apache Handlers*, then check out these two links:

- http://httpd.apache.org/docs/2.2/handler.html
- http://docs.cpanel.net/twiki/bin/view/AllDocumentation/CpanelDocs/ApacheHandlers

Image Manager

The Image Manager allows you to view and modify images in your account. You can change the size of your images, convert their file types, or just view them. Since you're using WordPress, you can manage your images much easier using the "Media" tab within your WordPress dashboard.

Index Manager

When accessing a directory (rather than a page) on your site, a visitor will typically see the index page for that directory. If no index page exists, the browser will display a list (or index) of the files in that directory.

Using the Index Manager, it is possible to define how a specific directory index will appear to those who access it. You can also turn off indexing, if you don't want a directory's contents to be visible. You can leave the default settings the way they are for the index manager.

Error Pages

An error page informs a visitor when there is a problem accessing your site. Each type of problem has its own code. For example, a visitor who enters a nonexistent URL will see a 404 error, while an unauthorized user trying to access a restricted area of your site will see a 401 error.

Basic error pages are automatically provided by the web server (Apache). However, if you prefer, you can **create a custom error page** for any valid HTTP status code beginning in 4 or 5.

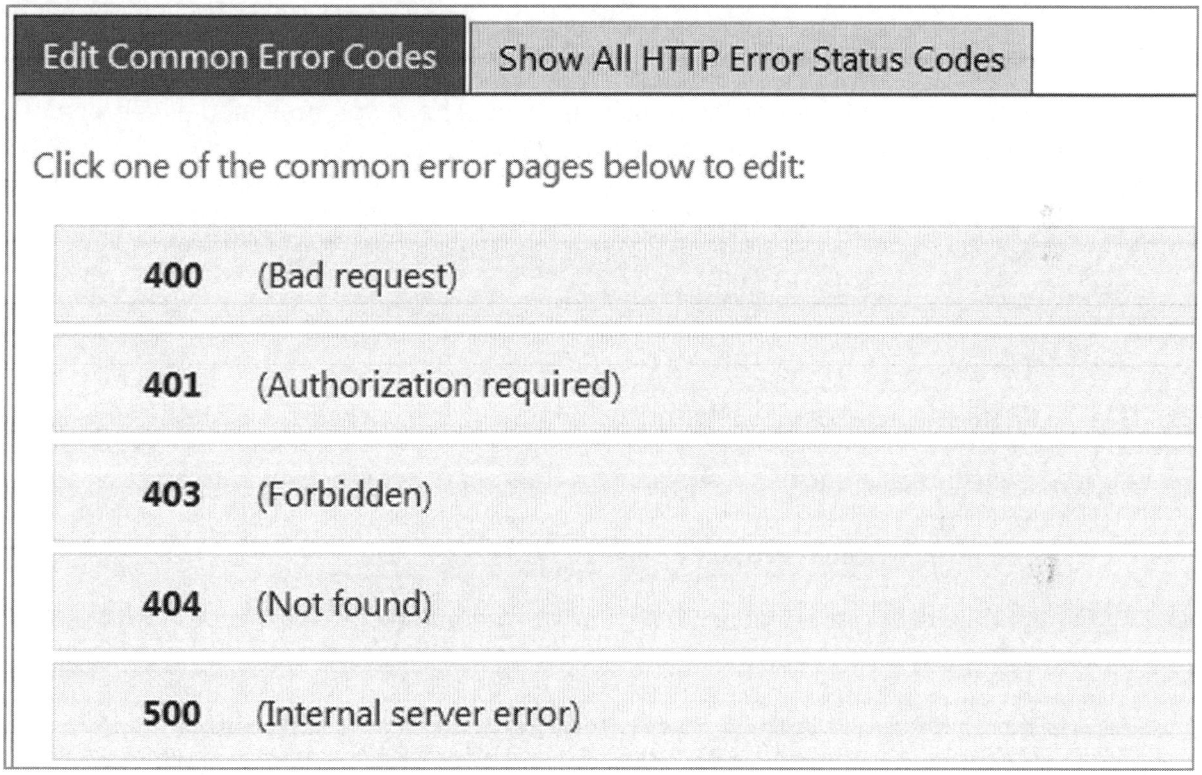

Edit Common Error Codes | Show All HTTP Error Status Codes

Click one of the common error pages below to edit:

400 (Bad request)

401 (Authorization required)

403 (Forbidden)

404 (Not found)

500 (Internal server error)

The most common error page that your visitors *might* get is a "**404 Error Page Not Found**." This will happen if you create a page, and then delete it later. If someone clicks on an old link that directs them to a page that you deleted, they'll get a *404 Error* page.

Ideally you don't want a *404 Error* page at all, so there's no need to create a custom message for such a page. *404 Error* pages are bad for search engine optimization because Google is linking to a page that doesn't exist. I recommend that you download a WordPress plugin that will redirect users to your homepage if they click on an old nonexistent URL.

Cron Jobs

Cron jobs allow you to automate certain commands or scripts on your site. You can set a command or script to run at a specific time every day, week, etc. For example, you could set a cron job to delete temporary files every week to free up disk space. The demo version of Bluehost's cPanel also runs a cron job to reset the dashboard since people create database users and email accounts on the demo account.

You'll see a warning explaining that you need to have a good knowledge of Linux commands before you can use cron jobs effectively. Check your script with your hosting administrator before adding a cron job.

Server Status

The "server status" icon will forward you to a page that'll keep you informed of server outages and other general system alerts affecting your server.

If you have multiple accounts, you can enter each one using the form on the page and a status message will appear for each account. You can also remove them from the list using the link that says "Remove Status Monitoring."

Process Manager

This feature displays the processes running on your server in a table over 6 columns:

1. **Pid** - The process identity. This is a unique number that is assigned to any process running on your server. You may click the process ID number to access 2 options: *trace* or *kill* the selected process.

2. **Owner** - The user or system account that started and owns the corresponding process.

3. **Priority** - This is a number between *-20* and *20* which tells how much time the system spends working on the process. -20 is the least CPU intensive, while 20 is the most.

4. **Cpu%** - The percentage of your server's processing power that the process is using.

5. **Mem%** - The percentage of RAM (memory) that the process is using on your server.

6. **Command** - Specifies the directory from which the CPU is receiving instructions.

404 Settings

After you click the "404 Settings" icon, you'll get forwarded to your account settings page. On this page you'll have the option to choose if you want to display advertisements on your

404 Error page. You'll also notice that you'll have the option to choose which page you'll see after you log into your cPanel dashboard.

Additionally you'll see an option to choose your web hosting renewal options. You'll see a disclaimer telling you that auto renewals take place 15 days before the end of your term. Month-to-month plans renew 24 hours before the month end.

MIME Types

The last icon within the advanced section says "MIME Types." MIME types tell browsers how to handle specific extensions. For example, the text/html MIME type equates to **.htm**, **.html**, and **.shtml** extensions on most servers, and this tells your browser to interpret all files with those extensions as HTML files.

You can alter or add new MIME types specifically for your site (*note that you cannot alter the system defined MIME type values*). MIME types are often used to handle **new technologies** as they appear.

All the MIME types you'll need are already created for you. Unless you're developing some new technology with new extensions, there's no need for you to create a new MIME Type.

Go Daddy Advanced Features

Go Daddy doesn't have a section for advanced features. Most people use shared hosting because it's simple, easy to use, and everything is already set up and ready to go.

Go Daddy does offer a *Cron Job* manager. Just log into your hosting account, click the "launch" button on the Web Hosting row, and then click on the "Cron Job Manager" icon. You'll get redirected to a page that'll allow you to easily create cron jobs by clicking the "Create" button on the top right of the screen.

That covers all of the advanced features within your cPanel dashboard. In the next chapter I'll discuss the "website builder tools" including the WordPress *one-click install* feature.

Chapter 11

Website Builders

The "website builders" section of cPanel is where you'll find the *one-click install* feature for WordPress. The very first icon you'll see will be a *WordPress* icon, and you can click the icon to start the step-by-step process.

WordPress

You can install WordPress on your domain name in less than 10 minutes. The only thing you need to do is:

- Select the domain name that you want to install WordPress on.
- Choose a username and password for WordPress.
- Then your hosting provider will automatically create a new database and install the software for you.

Simple Scripts

The next icon you'll see will say "Script Installs." If you click on that icon you'll see an entire list of different scripts that you can install on your domain including WordPress. You can also click the link that says "View My Installs" to see a listing of your currently installed scripts. You'll see your current WordPress installations on this page along with a few different options. You'll have the option to:

- See which version of WordPress you're using
- Upgrade your WordPress installation to the most current version
- Uninstall WordPress from your domain
- Manage some advanced features
- Reset your Password
- Log into your WordPress dashboard

Depending on your web host, you might not see a *WordPress* icon or the *Simple Scripts* option. Some web hosts will have an option called Quick Install or Fantastico. These are all auto installers that'll have the WordPress "one-click install" feature too.

goMobi

goMobi will help you transform your website into an easy to use mobile website. This is an add-on feature that'll cost $2.99/month per domain. Depending on your web host, you may or may not see this feature. Some of the advantages of goMobi are:

- Simple and easy set up
- No coding required
- Automatically redirects customers on a mobile device to your mobile site.
- Customers can contact you with one click.

Depending on your business, this might be a useful feature that you can take advantage of. They even have a YouTube video explaining how it works, and they'll show you a comparison with and without goMobi.

Mojo Market Place

The next section under *website builders* says "Mojo Market Place." All the icons in this section will take you to the same exact screen. Mojo Market Place is where you can install WordPress with one-click, so this section of cPanel is the same as the "Websites Builders" section.

It's important to note that you can buy **professional WordPress themes** using the Mojo Market Place. Just click the link at the top that says "themes" and click on the WordPress option to see themes that are compatible with WordPress.

The average WordPress theme will cost in-between $35 - $45. If you'd like to view free WordPress themes, then go to WordPress.org and click "themes" on the top menu. You can also search Google for free themes as well.

Go Daddy Website Builders

If you're using Go Daddy, you can find the WordPress *one-click install* feature easily. Click the "launch" button on the web hosting section, and the first icon you'll see says "WordPress."

If you're curious and you want to see other popular apps available through Go Daddy, then click the link that says "Show All" on the top left.

In the next chapter we'll talk about upgrades, professional services, and some other professional features within cPanel that you might find useful.

Chapter 12

Upgrades, Professional Services, and Promotional Extras

Within the "upgrades" section of cPanel you'll see items we've already discussed along with some new features. Depending on your web host you might see different options within the *upgrades* section. I'll focus on the most common upgrades that every web host offers, and I'll briefly discuss the other features that you may or may not have.

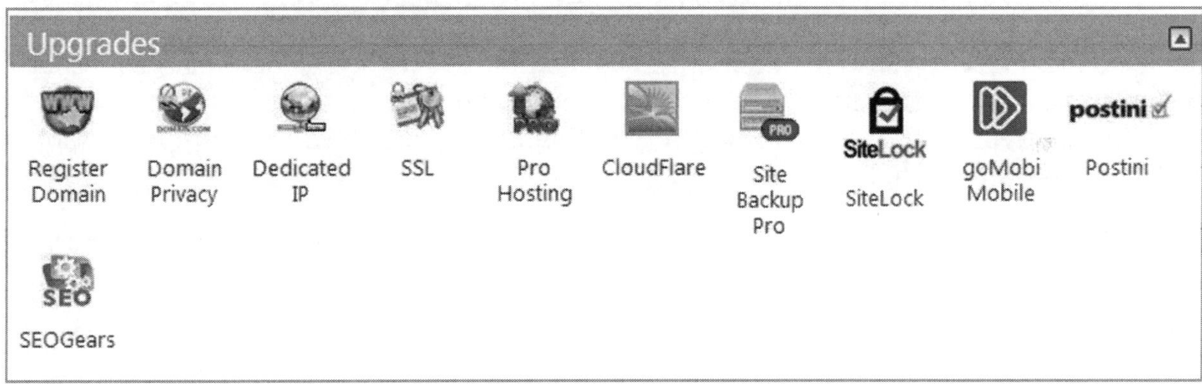

Domain Privacy

Currently the *Internet Corporation for Assigned Names and Numbers* (ICANN) broadly requires that the mailing address, phone number and e-mail address of those owning or administrating a domain name to be made **publicly available** through the "WHOIS" directories.

The domain owner's contact details, such as address and telephone number, are easily accessible to anyone who queries a *WHOIS* server. Spammers, direct marketers, identity thieves, or other attackers go through this directory looking for personal information about these people.

Although ICANN has been exploring changing *WHOIS* to enable greater privacy, no changes have been made yet. Domain registrars offer private registrations (also known as domain privacy), by which the contact information of the registrar is shown instead of the customer's. With the offer of "private registration" from many registrars, some of the risk has been mitigated.

I always highly recommend that you purchase domain privacy. As a business owner it's very important to *protect your personal "WHOIS" information from harvesting by solicitors and marketing companies*. The cost for privacy per domain is $9.99/year. If you don't purchase the domain privacy, you're going to receive a lot of SPAM email and junk mail to your home address.

Dedicated IP

A dedicated IP address might useful depending on your situation. The most common uses for a dedicated IP address are:

- Avoid Negative Impact from Others - On a dedicated IP you avoid possible negative action taken against shared IP users should someone on the same server get blocked.
- Enable SSL on Your Website - SSL Certificates are crucial if you have a business-oriented website and want to collect sensitive information.

Dedicated IP subscriptions are automatically synchronized with your hosting account term and expiration. For example, If you had a 12-month hosting subscription with 9 months remaining, when ordering a Dedicated IP you would only be billed the pro-rated amount for 9 months of Dedicated IP service.

A dedicated IP address can cost anywhere from $40-$70/year. Some web hosts will give you a free dedicated IP address when you purchase an SSL certificate from them.

SSL Certificates

SSL Certificates allow secure connections from a web server to a browser. Typically, SSL is used to secure credit card transactions, data transfer and logins, and more recently is becoming the norm when securing browsing of social media sites.

If you're going to collect credit card payments on your website, then you're going to need an SSL certificate. If you click on the SSL certificate icon, you'll have to option to purchase different types of SSL certificates. The price can range from $49 - $299/year. If you're not sure which SSL certificate you'll need, then contact your web host for assistance.

Additional Upgrades

Depending on your web host, the other upgrades you see within cPanel might be different. You'll notice some icons within the "upgrades" section that you've previously seen within cPanel. For example, with Bluehost you'll see CloudFlare, Site Backup Pro, goMobi, and Postini again.

You'll also see an upgrade called *Site Lock*, and you'll see another upgrade called *SEO Gears*. The **Site Lock** feature will provide you with:

- Basic Spam Monitoring
- Basic Business Verification

- Basic Malware Monitoring
- Site Verification Certificate
- Blacklist Monitoring

Site Lock will cost in between $19 - $199/year depending on your needs. The **SEO Gears** upgrade will offer you:

- Rapid Indexing
- Head-to-Head Competitive Analysis Report
- Search Engine Mastery EBook
- 12-Month Step-by-Step DIY SEO Program (Premium)

SEO Gears costs in-between $29-$99/year per domain name. This upgrade is definitely not worth the price. They are plenty of free tools and inexpensive books online that you can use to accomplish the same tasks.

Professional Services

The "professional services" section of cPanel offers some very useful features! The very first icon you'll see will say "Website Transfer." This is a very useful service if you want to move your website from another hosting company to your current hosting provider.

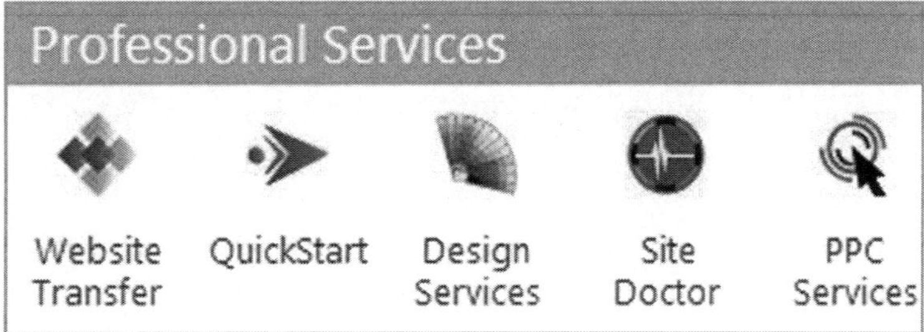

Website Transfer

For only $99 you'll get a team of professionals to:

- Transfer of up to 5 websites
- Migration of up to 20 email accounts
- Completion in a few days
- Review your site before it goes live

I've transferred a website by myself before, so trust me when I say it's not worth your time. It's 100% better to pay your web host to transfer your website for you while you focus on other aspects of your business. It'll take you days or even weeks to get everything set up and working correctly by yourself.

Quick Start

The next icon you'll see will say "Quick Start." If you click that icon, you'll get forwarded to a page that will offer you a quick coaching session for $29.99. This service includes a 45 minute phone call with a Bluehost expert that'll give you a "cPanel walk through."

The expert over the phone will also show you how to install WordPress and set up your email using cPanel. The good news is that I've already showed you how to install WordPress and set up your email accounts. I'm also giving you a step-by-step "cPanel walk through" right now; so I just saved you $29.99 minus the cost of this book. If you've made it this far in the book, then you won't need the *Quick Start* service.

Design Services

The next icon you'll see will say "Design Services." I don't advise paying for any website design services especially if you're going to use WordPress. You can easily design a website yourself if you're using the WordPress platform.

If you click on the *design services* link, you'll notice that their cheapest package is $49/month and it's a 24 month service. That's about $1,200 and that doesn't even include hosting fees. I think that's way too expensive and I recommend that you buy a book on the subject instead.

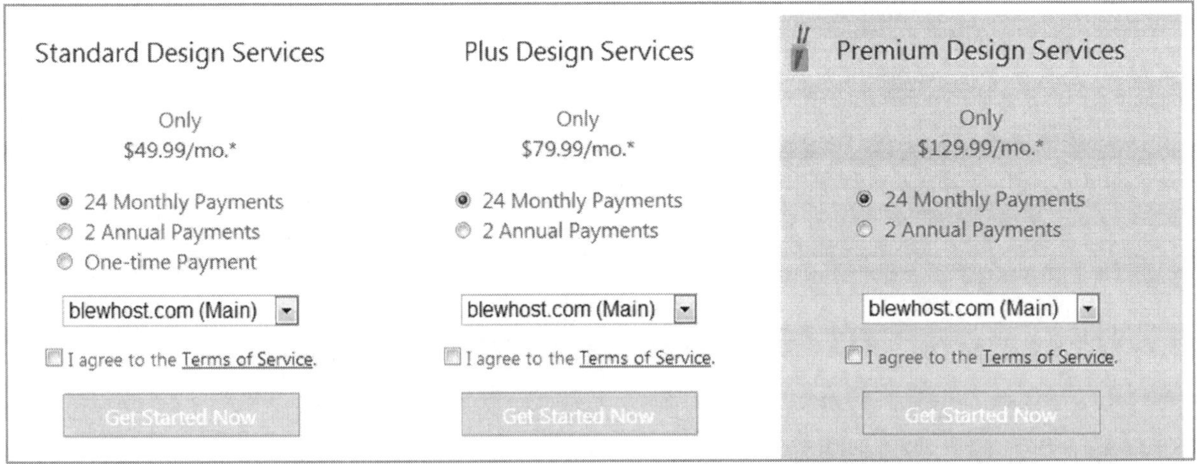

We have books teaching you how to build a website with WordPress and Search Engine Optimization (SEO). If you like this book so far, then you'll find our other books useful too.

Site Doctor

If your website gets hacked often, then you might want to give the "Site Doctor" a call. I highly recommend this service if someone keeps hacking into your site and changing things around. For $49.99 you'll receive:

- Security Scan - Scan your entire website for malicious code (hacks, malware, and viruses).
- Malware Removal - Remove any malicious files/code that's found.
- Security Consultation - They'll discuss possible vulnerabilities and advise on how to further secure your website.
- Clean Site Guarantee - Guarantees a clean site for 30 days. They'll promptly clean any re-infection within 30 days at no additional cost.
- Version Control – They'll log any changes they make, and you can undo them if you choose.
- Software Update - Any *Simple Scripts* programs you've installed will be updated to the latest, most secure versions.

PPC Service

PPC stands for **Pay Per Click**. The advertisements you see at the *top* and *right* hand side of Google are PPC ads. The advertiser only pays for the ad when someone clicks on the advertisement link.

If you'd like your hosting company to run PPC campaigns for you, then click on the *PPC Service* icon and select your monthly budget for advertisements. If you'd like to do your own PPC advertising, then you go to directly through **Google Adwords** or **Bing Ads**.

Promotional

The last section within cPanel has some promotional credits that you can use to advertise your website. Most web hosts will offer you free advertisement credits to help you *jump start* your website.

Bluehost offers advertisement credits with Google AdWords, Twitter, Facebook, and a free listing with the Yellow Pages. If you click the "more" link, you'll see additional business tools, services, web design templates, and affiliate partners that you can use to help you run an E-commerce website.

The promotional items you'll see within your cPanel dashboard will be different depending on your web host. Most web hosts will at least offer you a $100 credit for Google Adwords. If you decide to set up a Google Adwords account, make sure that you fully understand how the program works.

Google AdWords is PPC (pay per click) marketing which means you'll get charged every time someone clicks on your advert. You'll have to register your credit card when you sign up with Google Adwords.

After your free $100 credit runs out, Google will start to automatically bill your credit card. If you don't set a daily advertisement budget, or you forget that you have ads running on Google, you could easily max-out your credit card in less than a day. If you're new to advertising online, make sure that you know exactly how a specific advertising platform works **before** you enter your credit card information.

Go Daddy Upgrades, Professional Services, and Other Tools

To find upgrades for your website you'll have to click the "launch" button on the *domains* row. You'll see a list of your domain names and you'll need to click on the domain name that you want to assign upgrades too. You'll get forwarded to a page that'll allow you to manage your domain name.

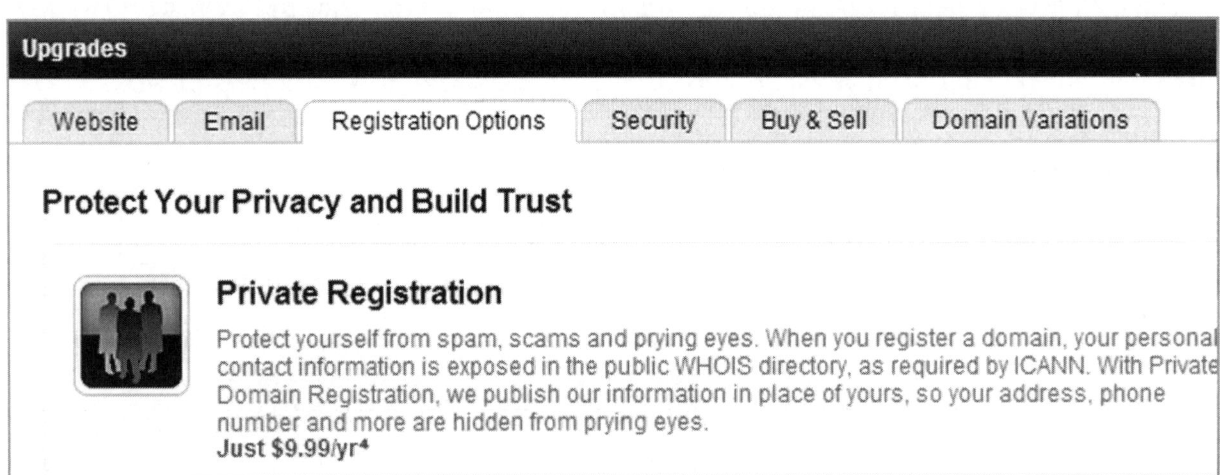

Click the button that says "Upgrade" on the menu under your domain name and you'll see different tabs that'll offer upgrades such as:

- **Private Registration** - With Private Domain Registration, Go Daddy will publish their information in place of yours, so your address, phone number and more are hidden from the WHOIS directory.
- **Business Registration** - Add your business name, logo, phone number, hours of operation, photos, and even a map to your WHOIS listing.
- **Deluxe Registration** - Get Private Registration combined with Business Registration. Make your business details available in the WHOIS directory while your personal information remains hidden.
- **Protected Registration** - Deluxe Registration plus safeguards against expiration and accidental or malicious transfer with *Deadbolt Transfer Protection* services. Includes both Private Registration and Business Registration.
- **Certified Domain** - A Certified Domain Validation Seal shows visitors that your site is trustworthy by authenticating your domain and placing a dynamic seal on your home page
- **SSL Certificates** - Secure the data transmitted to and from your site — including credit card numbers, usernames, passwords and more.
- **Auction Memberships** – If you're interested in buying and selling domain names.
- **Premium Listings** – List your domain name for sale where millions of people can see it.
- **CashParking** – Make money from your parked domain names that you're not using with Go Daddy advertisements.
- **Domain Variations** – Protect your online brand and identity by registering similar name variations. (i.e different domain name extensions like .net, .org, .info, .biz, etc...)

More Tools and Promotions for Go Daddy

If you click the "launch" button on the web hosting row, you'll see a few tools within your dashboard that are not available with Bluehost and a lot of other hosts. Go Daddy has an icon that says Sitemaps.

Sitemaps

You can easily create a sitemap by clicking the box next to your domain and click the "Create" button on the top menu. Sitemaps help ensure that all new and difficult-to-find pages are indexed quickly and completely by search engines like Google.

Sitemaps are particularly useful for websites that are difficult for search engines to crawl and index effectively. You can also access crawl statistics, recent queries, errors, and other information that Google has collected about your site using the *Google's Webmaster Tools* feature.

Google Webmasters Tools

Click the "Google Webmasters Tool" icon to make your site more "Google-friendly" with Google's free webmaster tools. This feature will show you Google's view of your website, help you diagnose site issues, and allow you share information with Google to help improve your site's visibility in search results.

You'll have to verify your website first. You can verify your website by clicking the box next to the site(s) you want to verify and then click the "verify" button on the top menu. Just follow the step-by-step instructions to get set up. For more information about Google Webmaster Tools, you can visit their official website at: http://google.com/webmasters/tools/

Password Vault

If you want a secure place to store all your passwords for FTP accounts, WordPress websites, Emails, etc, you can use the "Password Vault" feature. You'll need to know your FTP password to access this feature.

Password Vault

Add New Password to Vault

Application User Name Password

Add Password

After you enter your FTP password, you'll be able to manage your username and passwords for multiple applications. You'll have the option to enter the name of the application along with the matching username and password.

This is a very useful feature to help keep you organized. There are paid membership websites that are dedicated to helping you keep track of your usernames and passwords, but it's a free feature with Go Daddy.

Advertising Credits

Go Daddy has free advertisement credits too for Google Adwords, Facebook, Bing, Yahoo, and Fotolia. From the main dashboard you have to click the "Payments" tab, and then click the link that says "Advertising Credits" on the left menu.

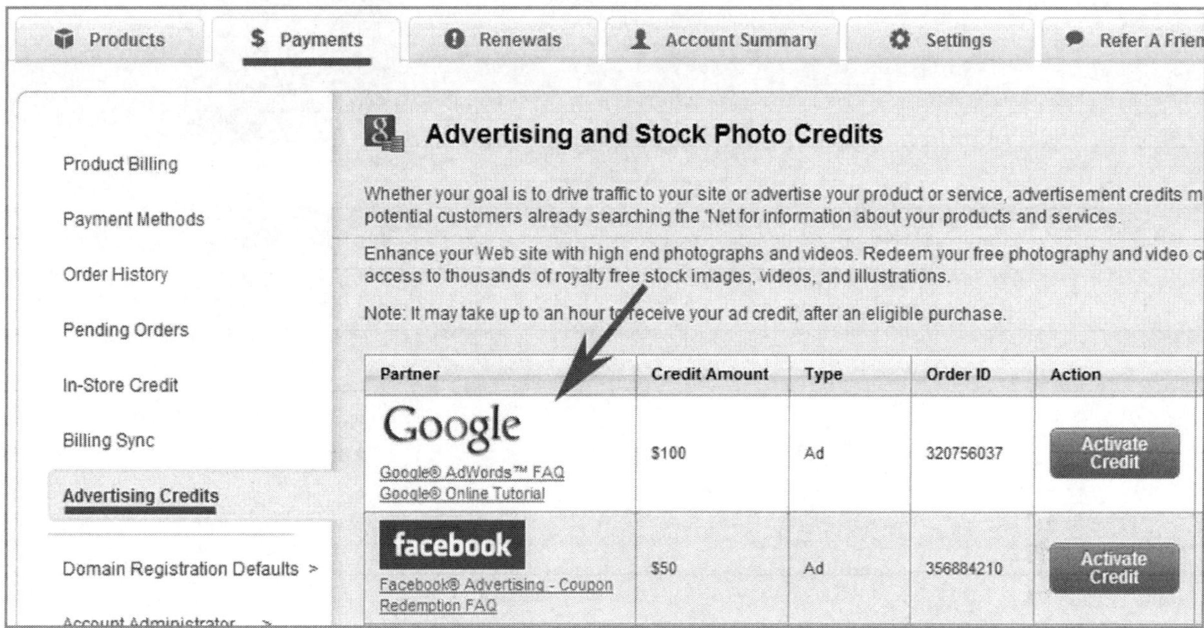

You'll see the available advertising partners that Go Daddy works with along with the credit amount. Click the "Activate" button to activate the credit and follow the easy instructions to use the advertising credits.

More Products and Services

Go Daddy has way too many products to cover in this book. They have website builder services, website protection scanners, online storage tools, SEO services, and a lot more. To find these products, click on the "All Products" menu and look through all the sub-menus to see all the available products and services.

All Products
Cart
Find Yo
Domai
All Products
Domains
Hosting & Servers
Storage
Web Design
Improve your Business
Email
SSL & Security
Auctions
Small Business Center
My Account
Mobile A
My Help

Chapter 13

Brief Summary and Conclusion

Your *cPanel* and *Hosting Control Center* should be a lot easier to understand now. Some companies will charge you thousands of dollars to help set up and manage your hosting account, but you can easily do this yourself.

You've probably noticed that I didn't discuss the "top menu" on your cPanel dashboard. The reason I skipped the top menu is because those links are **shortcuts** to areas we've already discussed.

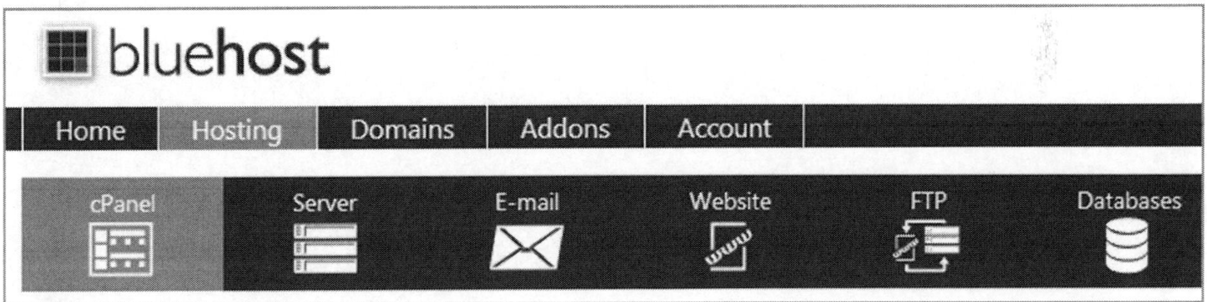

Please click though all the links on to top menu so you'll feel confident that I'm not leaving anything out.

Summary

The top three WordPress web hosts I recommend are:

1. Bluehost
2. GoDaddy
3. InMotion

As I mentioned earlier, most web hosts will be able to host a simple WordPress website because WordPress doesn't require that many resources. The WordPress hosting providers I've recommended are:

- Well established
- Have excellent customer support
- Have WordPress trained technicians
- Offer a vast amount of **upgrades** and **special tools** to help improve your websites performance.

You should always do your own research before you decide on a WordPress hosting provider. If you'd like to see a large list of cPanel partners, then you might find this link useful: http://cpanel.net/hosting-providers/hosting-provider-showcase/

If you have additional questions, please feel free to contact us for a helping hand. If you'd like to learn more about creating a WordPress website or blog, then please check out our other WordPress training guides. Have a good day, and I wish you success with your website!

-Matthew Pitt & Kent Mauresmo

http://BestWebHostingInc.com

http://Read2Learn.net

Glossary

Add-on Domain: Another website with its own unique content. You'll have to register the new domain name before you can host it.

Apache Handlers: Handlers tell the web server how to handle certain types of files (html, cgi, pl, etc.)

Bandwidth: A measure of how much data is transferred to or from your website, email, or FTP accounts. Typically, this is measured in computer gigabytes (GB).

cPanel: A popular web-based hosting control software to help you easily manage your website.

Cron Jobs: Commands or web scripts that the web server executes at a particular time.

Database: Databases are used to store information for quick retrieval. Many web scripts require at least one database. WordPress requires a database. MySQL and PostgreSQL are used to manage databases.

Dedicated Server: An entire web server to that's not shared with anyone else. You can use a dedicated server to sell shared hosting accounts or whatever you want. This is the most expensive type of web hosting.

Disk Space: This is the measure of how much stuff you can store on a server or in your hosting account. Disk space is usually measured in computer megabytes (MB).

DNS (Domain Name Service): The system that allows domain names to be translated into their corresponding IP addresses.

Domain Name: The name of a website or location on the internet. A domain name resolves to an IP address via DNS.

DOS (Denial of Service) Attack: This sort of attack uses many computers to flood your web server with fake requests for information with the hope of taking the server or your site off the internet.

FrontPage Extensions: Special code that runs on a web server to enable additional features in Microsoft's FrontPage HTML editor program. Do not enable the FrontPage extensions unless you plan to use Microsoft FrontPage exclusively to edit your website.

FTP (File Transfer Protocol): A protocol for transferring and working with files and directories on a remote server.

FTP Client: A program used to work with files on a remote server via FTP or SFTP. (i.e. Filezilla)

Hit: A request for a web page or other content on your website.

HTML: The programming language most web pages are written in.

Index Page: On most websites, the index page is the first page accessed when someone visits that domain.

IP Address: The number assigned to an item accessible on the Internet. IP addresses currently are a series of four "three-digit" numbers separated by periods (111.111.111.111).

Kernel: The core of the Linux operating system.

MIME Types: MIME stands for *Multipurpose Internet Mail Extensions.* MIME types let a user's web browser know what a given file is so that it knows how to handle that file.

Parked Domain: A domain that mirrors the content of the main domain managed in cPanel. With Go Daddy, a parked domain is a domain that you haven't built a website on yet. You'll just see Go Daddy advertisements on a Go Daddy parked domain.

Perl: A programming language used by some web scripts.

PHP: A programming language that a lot of web-based scripts use.

phpMyAdmin: Web-based program that allows you to manipulate MySQL databases.

phpPgAdmin: Web-based program that allows you to manipulate PostgreSQL databases.

Ping: The amount of time (milliseconds) that it takes for a server to respond to a request. The longer times mean the connection will be slower.

Raw Web Log: The log created by Apache as user's access websites on the web server.

Redirect: A redirect sends anyone who accesses a web page to a new location.

SFTP: A secure encrypted version of the FTP protocol.

Shared Hosting: Many websites hosted on a single web server.

SSL (Secure Socket Layer): SSL is sometimes referred to as TLS (Transport Layer Security). This is the main protocol used on the web to ensure that traffic to and from a website is encrypted so third parties cannot intercept important personal data like credit cards.

SSL Certificate: A special file that enables SSL communications between a website and the user's web browser.

Subdomains: Sub-domains are addresses like *maps.google.com*. A sub-domain can either act as if it were an entirely different site, or a shortcut to redirect you to another place in your site or anywhere on the internet.

VPS Hosting: VPS stands for *Virtual Private Server*. VPS hosting accounts use special software to take a single physical server and divide it into 2 or more virtual web servers. Each virtual server acts as if it's a completely separate machine. VPS hosting is a great alternative to "Dedicated" web hosting because it's cost effective and offers similar features.

Web Scripts: Programs that run via a web browser over the internet.

Web Server: A machine that serves web pages and other content on the internet. Also the software (like Apache) that actually does the serving.

Web Stat Program: A program like *Webalizer* or *AWSTATS* that interprets the raw data in the Apache raw web logs and condenses that information into useful charts and graphs.

Web Statistics: Basic information about where your visitors came from, how they found your site and what sort of computer and browser they used during the visit. The information comes from the Apache raw web log.

Webmaster: The person responsible for the content and running of a website.....YOU!

Acknowledgments

*The authors want to acknowledge the main person that helped make this book a reality; and her name is **Lila H. Vegas**. She conducted almost 1000 surveys just because she wanted to help. The surveys she conducted enabled us to address the most frequently asked questions in regards to WordPress web hosting. Thank you for your help!*

More Books From The Authors

You can find more books from the authors on Amazon by following the link below:
amazon.com/author/read2learn

29952147R00076

Made in the USA
Middletown, DE
08 March 2016